ALESSI

ALESSI
THE DESIGN FACTORY

A.D. ACADEMY EDITIONS

Art & Design Monographs
Editorial Office: 42 Leinster Gardens, London W2 3AN

Edited by: Meret Gabra-Liddell
Art Editor: Andrea Bettella
House Editor: Nicola Hodges
Editorial and Design Team: Rachel Bean, Meret Gabra-Liddell, Laurence Scelles

All photographic material supplied by Il Quadrifoglio; except pp36-37 courtesy of
Atelier Hollein; pp140-43 Pentagram (Richard Davies)

Acknowledgements: We would like to thank everyone who has contributed to this
monograph, particularly Ausilia Fortis at Alessi spa; all the architects and designers who
have provided material for publication; and Steven Kysfin at the Royal College of Art for
his kind assistance with Daniel Weil's essay, and Jeremy Myerson for editing it.

COVER: Alberto Alessi with '100% Vases' and the trolley from Casa della Felicità; PAGE 2: The Alessi
Family with Philippe Starck's 'Juicy Salif'

First published in Great Britain in 1994 by
ACADEMY EDITIONS
An imprint of the Academy Group Ltd

ACADEMY GROUP LTD
42 Leinster Gardens London W2 3AN
Member of VCH Publishing Group

ISBN 1 85490 334 9

Distributed to the trade in the United States of America by
ST MARTIN'S PRESS
175 Fifth Avenue, New York, NY 10010

Printed and bound in Singapore

CONTENTS

FUN FACTORY
MERET GABRA-LIDDELL

 The most striking thing about gathering the material for this book has been the feeling of fun, happiness and creativity which surrounds and touches everything and everyone involved with Alessi. Every person I have spoken to has sung the praises of the company and of Alberto Alessi himself. When I finally met him I understood why. He is the Circus Master: he is fun, witty, dynamic and charming, and it is this side of his character which has kept the Alessi company growing from strength to strength.

Critics say that Alessi typified the eighties 'design decade' and that there is no place for their products in the 'caring sharing' nineties. But Alessi has again risen beyond the critics. Their philosophy is that of a 'design factory', a hotbed of creative ideas, making the company function more as a collective of designers, such as those seen at the beginning of this century – the Secessionists, Wiener Werkstätte, Bauhaus and the Arts and Crafts movement to name a few – rather than as a purely industrial production line.

The layout of this book is one of a thematic chronology. Like any other life form the Alessi company has its own genealogy, due to the design process initiated by Alberto Alessi – the Metaproject – the products do have a life of their own. They create new gene pools which when combined create new life forms – products – thus creating new branches and new species.

The Alessi experimentation started in earnest when Alberto met what he calls the 'maestros': Achille Castiglioni, Ettore Sottsass, Richard Sapper and Alessandro Mendini. These four masters of design taught, guided, designed and encouraged Alberto to follow his imagination and push back the boundaries of industrial design. The design diversification began and it has moved and multiplied with its own momentum over the last two decades, expanding into various offshoots of the main Alessi line: Officina, the experimentation umbrella; Twergi, products in wood; Tendentse, ceramics; and Centro Studi Alessi, research and development.

The influence of Rossi, Graves, Venturi and Starck is also not to be underestimated, as they are, in Alberto's words 'the new maestros'. They work closely and productively with the company and, in the case of Graves, have produced an entire family of products which will carry on developing.

The inclusion of a section on Programme 8 in the brief history chapter, typifies the early attempts at experimentation and the influence of the young Alberto on the direction of the company. Not content with producing practical and beautiful products, Alberto took example from his father and involved designers in projects (Massoni and Mazzeri's cocktail set, 1957), and commissioned two designers, Franco Sargiani and Eija Helander, to redesign the concept of tableware from first principles. This was an incredible project encompassing the design and philosophical ideas that were later to emerge in the development of new lines and products.

Alessi never does things by halves. There are workshops, metaprojects, seminars, lectures and philosophical discussions in abundance generating prototypes and a 'Not in Production' list almost as big as their main lines.

Through its Centro Studi, Alessi is encouraging the growth of new talent with workshops such as 'Memory Containers', bringing together new designers in brainstorming design sessions, the final results of which are incorporated into the main Alessi line.

Alberto has also initiated projects in various schools of design around Europe, with a programme of lectures to students of industrial design. His philosophy and stress on the need for good design has become a personal crusade, where his sense of fun and wit is passed on to an equally enthusiastic audience making his design projects some of the most interesting and entertaining parts of demanding curriculums.

This creativity will carry the company forward: the ability to change, to experiment, to diversify, to respond to social, political and economical vagaries will allow the company to maintain their reputation as the best and most ingenious manufacturers of household goods.

There must be a place for the Alessi company in the future because no place that is so happy, and gives so much happiness, should be lost. As Alberto Alessi says 'the "House of Happiness" was intended as a house of happy projects, an authentic project, well conceived, free, strong, a manifestation of a theme very dear to Alessi'. The Alessi company is indeed the 'Fun Factory'.

OPPOSITE BACKGROUND IMAGE: 'Girotondo' tray, King Kong, 1989-90; *INSET: Riccardo Dalisi, Neopolitan coffee maker, prototypes, 1979-87*

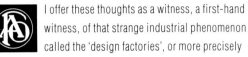

THE DESIGN FACTORIES EUROPE'S INDUSTRIAL FUTURE?

ALBERTO ALESSI

I offer these thoughts as a witness, a first-hand witness, of that strange industrial phenomenon called the 'design factories', or more precisely the 'Italian design factories'.

The origins of the Alessi family business, of which I am now one of the two chairmen, lie with my two grandfathers: the maternal one, Alfonso Bialetti, and the paternal one, Giovanni Alessi. They are both heirs of the very old artisan tradition of producing small wooden and metal objects typical of the Strona Valley, a narrow mountain valley near to Lake Orta in the Italian Alps, close to Switzerland. My two grandfathers pursued different directions as producers. In the thirties Grandfather Bialetti invented, designed and manufactured the octagonal coffee maker in cast aluminium which became so famous after the war: a true object of mass production. Grandfather Alessi started the Alessi company in 1921 which produced a wide variety of different objects for the table in brass and nickel silver. While to this day the Bialetti company has continued to manufacture just one product – the octagonal coffee maker – producing around four million pieces a year, the Alessi company has produced many thousands of different objects during more or less the same period. Today there are around 2,000 different items in our catalogues.

The Bialetti and Alessi companies began to take on very different shapes (or different natures?) during the fifties . . . I have to confess that the Bialetti company has always conjured up images of the assembly lines in the Charlie Chaplin film *Modern Times*, whereas Alessi was, and is today, a kind of handicraft made with the help of machines. How strange this is, since my two grandparents shared the same kind of passion for their work, for skilful handmade work. I remember well when I visited their workshops, as a child. What a difference in terms of industry, and in a way how confusing for me to try to understand, especially as I was a little child!

This premise is simply to say that I find it difficult to clearly define the difference between 'industry' and 'handicraft' . . . not to mention what the strange word 'design' really means: I don't actually believe that we can give a universal definition to this word, that is a definition which is accepted by everybody. For instance, I have always been equally attracted by the two opposite versions, Mies van der Rohe's 'less is more', and Robert Venturi's 'more is not less, less is a bore'. However, I'll try to do my best.

I started work at Alessi with a premise that was important to me, a premise which is still valid today: I didn't believe that industry in general had reached a definitive stage in its development, a perfect shape that prevented further, and maybe at the time, unforeseeable modifications in its way of thinking, acting and organising in the social context. On the contrary, I was convinced that the way to conceive and to organise production – to think of products, to offer them on the market, to keep people working and communicate their activity – could be greatly modified in the future. Maybe it hasn't been so far, it all depends on us.

I was also convinced, because of my classical and philosophical education, that the consumer society wouldn't be the last stage of the 'well-being society' in which we happily live. It is probably the most progressive stage humanity has ever reached, but it is destined to evolve into a way of life where products will have less importance and Man will have much more. Yes, when I started working at Alessi, in 1970, maybe I was a little too Utopian!

The Role of Objects in Consumer Society

I also had some convictions, some philosophical thoughts, on the role of objects in our actual society, the consumer society. We live in a society where all the relevant material needs are fulfilled by the production of objects, but the big mass production industry didn't seem to have understood this. I believed – I believe – that in most cases, mass production industry goes on working simply to satisfy people's needs, instead of paying more attention to their wishes, to their desires.

I intentionally use the word 'society' and not the word 'market', because today it seems that the management of mass production industries use market to mean a cage in which to try and force the dynamic reality of society (of what people really feel and want), rather than as an evolved cognitive model of society, as would be hoped. It seemed to me that at that time people were changing the way they wished to benefit from and enjoy objects, and I had – I have – the feeling that marketing, intended as something based above all on statistics and logic, couldn't give a clear enough interpretation.

Later on in my career, from the second half of the seventies onwards, I was very lucky to start working with many good architects and designers, who also became important maestros/teachers. They included Ettore Sottsass,

Richard Sapper, Achille Castiglioni and Alessandro Mendini. Working and discussing ideas with them, I started to feel something that became clear some years later through the 'laboratory' experience of our work at Alessi: that people buy our coffee makers and our kettles less because they need to make coffee or make the water boil, and more for other reasons. Just what these reasons are I will also consider.

I know that in saying this I will attract criticism from a certain kind of intelligentsia, in particular Anglo-Saxon, and I am well aware that during the last few years a certain kind of 'neo-functionalist' guidance always lies in wait, doesn't it? It is fitting that today there should be some rectifications to our guidelines, and that maybe some hedonistic aspects, typical of the eighties should be corrected. But I also think that to avoid the risk of doing some 'too-low-profile function-alism', one point should be clarified right away: speaking about Alessi products (small, mainly metal objects for the kitchen and home) we find ourselves working in a system where all the typologies are centuries or even millennia old; where the functional characteristics were acquired a long time ago and where it is nearly impossible to introduce important functional innovations. So the functional aspect exists, of course, but it is physiologically intrinsic to the projects. While I am convinced that there are other important aspects to be explored, not only using 'design' (design is perhaps a word which is not really sufficient to express what I want to say), but addressing a wider range of disciplines which I define in a broad sense as 'anthropological', encompassing such areas as my latest interests: semiology and psychology.

In our society objects have become the main channel through which we communicate information to others about our values, our status and our personality. The possession and use of objects essentially means an exchange of cultural and social meanings. Through the free choice of the objects which surround us, we invest in them an important social meaning, treating them as signs of our values to be communicated to everybody, in a visible and intelligible way (objects as signs of status or standing). But this is not all: I am convinced that people tend to use objects as a means to satisfy a hidden and fundamental need for 'art' and 'poetry'; a need which is no longer exclusively fulfilled by the traditional instruments of artistic exhibition (art in muse-ums, poetry in books), a need which stands out from society (and so from the market) and that industry, mass production industry, has not yet understood.

Design Factories versus Mass Production Factories

By managing projects, by producing objects, it slowly became clear to me that my activity, even if it was always a producer activity, was different from that of the so-called 'mass production industry'. I was far from one of the main and most worrying characteristics of mass production

industry (speaking on a medium to long-term basis): that of not taking risks. On the contrary, to be obliged to take risks was a physiological element of our activity. Not to take risks means that products tend inevitably to become more and more homogeneous, that their relative markets get saturated and that in consequence the factories become more and more troubled. For instance, look at what has happened in the automobile market: people seemed to have got tired of buying cars. Now, if it's true that cars, refrigerators and television sets are getting more and more homogeneous, this seems to be less true of what we call 'high design' and the factories practising it, what we could call the design factories (though this doesn't mean that this second type of industry hasn't got its problems, but their problems are different).

In exploring this difference it became clear to me that towards the end of this century two main ways of looking at design seem to be emerging, two different and sometimes contradictory visions. On one side, there is the interpreta-tion of design peculiar to mass production companies, where it is looked upon as one of the many marketing and technological tools. This interpretation tends to reduce the role of design, using it only as a tool to help industry produce more functional products, more rapidly, at lower costs, or to give a better 'look' to products, to invite people to buy. It is a 'gastronomic' vision of design, where design is looked upon as a sort of spice, more or less rare, as a seasoning to make our food tastier (our products more interesting).

This way of defining design, limiting it to one of the many marketing and technological tools, is not sufficient to explain the complex phenomenon of design today, nor to explain where design is going in the coming years. Moreover, if we look around we can see the results of this way of looking at design: a world of anonymous products, boring objects usually without emotions and without poetry.

Here I come to a second and very unique way of looking at design, a way very close to the approach of the Italian design factories: design intended as art and poetry. When I talk about the Italian design factories I refer to a number of companies which mainly developed in the post-war period. They constitute (with the exception of a few recent cases) a limited number of companies, some 20 or 30, which consider design as the central and basic element of their activity. According to these companies design is – let me use an exaggerated expression – a 'Mission'. It has less and less the meaning of a simple, formal project for an object; on the contrary, it has become a sort of 'general philosophy', of *Weltanschauung*, characterising all the decisions of these companies. This kind of company – generally private companies geared towards profit, acting in a capitalistic society to produce and sell goods to consumers, and very aware of the relationship between costs and benefits – are

very attentive to the fact that they live and act in the context of 'material culture', in a daily comparison with what we call Applied Arts.

The application of Applied Arts in everyday life is a century-old idea. It has been a topical theme since the Industrial Revolution, in particular during the second half of the last century, following the polemics waged by John Ruskin, William Morris and the Arts and Crafts Movement, against the growth of mass production. Morris – writer, painter, artist, entrepreneur and designer *ante litteram* – argued against the industry of his time producing bad taste and bad quality products, in contrast to the handicraft production which, in his opinion, was more spontaneous, of higher quality and more mindful of the artistic and cultural factors (a critical view of mass production which is also a constant in the case of the Italian design factories). In the following century, design seen as art and poetry took on other important forms and aspects: from the Arts and Crafts movements in England and America in the second part of the last century, to the Wiener Werkstätte in Vienna at the beginning of our century, the German Deutsche Werkbund, the Bauhaus in Weimar and Dessau in the twenties, the Ulm School in the fifties, up to the phenomenon of the Italian design factories born in the post-war years. In my opinion, we may consider the Italian design factories as the last spiritual heirs of these creative and intellectual movements which share a common concern to produce objects with a very strong cultural and intellectual feature. We believe that the fundamental nature of Alessi and its design ethos is closer to a research laboratory in the Applied Arts than to an industry in the canonic way; a research lab in Applied Arts where there is an endless mediation between the most advanced expressions of the creative culture and the public's requirements and dreams.

The 'Transgressing Component'

This research lab should be characterised by the greatest openness and availability in the world of creation, though the techniques offered by modern marketing are not helping us enough. And here we are at a *punctum dolens*. A possible point of friction between design as a global creative discipline and marketing as a science founded on statistics, may lie in the 'transgressing component' which in my opinion is an historical constant in Italian Design.

In order to clarify and expand upon this I will use an example taken from our activity: the Tea and Coffee Piazza operation. One must ask if Italian design has a particular characteristic, a constant factor which can be found in all its best examples and which enables us to recognise them in the richer and richer background of the international industrial production. I think this characteristic exists and arises from the transgressing component so evident in every

project which has become famous in the industrial culture of my country. The concept of 'transgression' implies the concept of 'rule'; and the 'rule-system' inside which industrial enterprise takes place can be divided into three groups. Firstly, there are technical-functional rules (which regulate the material production of objects); secondly, the socio-economic and marketing rules (which regulate the entry of objects onto the market); and thirdly, the aesthetic and communication rules (which regulate the comprehension and the acceptance of objects by people). But, and this is very important, a rule system also tends to imply a static vision of the world and probably – in the case of industry – a strong brake to evolution. In fact I believe that an excessive attention to the *pro tempore* current rules, indicated in each of the three previously mentioned groups, is leading to a progressive and dramatic fall in the creative intensity of many great international industries. I have already mentioned the automobile industry: I'm convinced that an important reason for people's loss of interest in cars, and for the unprecedented crisis which the car market is experiencing, is the fact that European and American cars are all very similar, copied from each other, boring, with no emotion, so that people prefer to keep their old car rather than spending a lot of money on another probably less exciting one. People don't like to take risks to be disappointed, and industries don't like to take the risk of true innovation. (There are other reasons regarding car design: the great insistence on a very functional aspect and the research into high-speed performance – yet what is the sense of designing faster and faster cars with all the existing speed limits? In my opinion it is a silly attempt to follow wishes.)

On the contrary, I believe that a gradual start to the transgression of these rules is not only acceptable, but is even to be hoped for. This transgressing component, this acceptance of the risk associated with the transgression of the rules in force, is one of the most typical features of the Italian design factories. Through this can be interpreted the main expressions of our design history, the ability to bring technology to its highest point: in Giò Ponti's super-light chair for Cassina, in Carlo Mollino's work, or Franco Albini's furniture for Arflex, or the objects by Marco Zanuso and Richard Sapper for Brionvega and Artemide. I am also referring to the desire to care nothing for the status-quo established by contemporary marketing, as Achille Castiglioni for Flos, Mario Bellini, Bruno Munari or Enzo Mari for Danese have demonstrated. Finally, I mean the wish to break from the ruling figurative tradition which typifies the 'Radical Design' phenomenon of the sixties and, during the past decade, of the Italian groups Alchimia and Memphis, with Ettore Sottsass, Alessandro Mendini and Andrea Branzi.

The curious thing is that these turmoils have often led to the production of objects which have been very well received

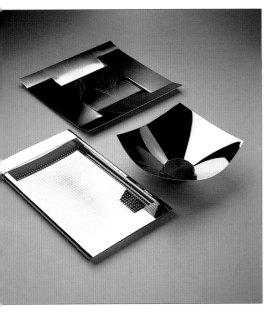

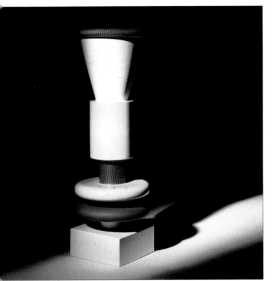

on the market. They have exhibited experimental tendencies which are then later adopted by much bigger industries than those which, at the beginning, financed these projects (Espace and its copies have been derived from a prototype elaborated by Mario Bellini for Cassina in the seventies.)

Design as Art and Poetry?

The reasoning which I use to support the premise that 'design is art and poetry' can be divided into two groups of thoughts. The first concerns the statement that design is a global creative discipline of artistic and poetic origin, and not simply one of the numerous tools available to marketing and technology for the production and better sales of industrial products. I will not miss the opportunity to repeat this affirmation, because it is still somewhat discouraging to consider the product policy generally pursued by mass production industry, which it seems to me has not grasped this fact at all. An interesting contribution here comes from the studies conducted by the British psychoanalyst DW Winnicott on 'transitional objects'. He identified, in the comprehensive area of human experience, a widely unknown zone situated between dreams and reality, halfway between things perceived and things conceived, neither inside nor outside the individual, which he called the 'area of transitional phenomena'. The objects that populate it, the transitional ones – games, teddy bears, the little boy Linus' blanket – are a sort of magic representation for the child of the happy sphere in which he was joined to his mother:

> . . . to these objects the child attaches himself while sleeping, to find comfort, an image of her which he can keep by him all the time, evoking the reassuring unity with his mother . . . and in this way the transitional objects produce the effect of obtaining precisely what it had set out to deny: it enables the mother to go out while the child keeps her close to him symbolically.[1]

Winnicott refers to the area of children's play, which begins with the child's first experience in this sense (with the use of transitional objects and games) but later also expands far beyond it, and continues in the adult's creative and cultural life. He thinks that the area of the transitional phenomena continues in the intense experience we find in religion, in all forms of artistic creation and fruition, and also in creative scientific work. The child's transitional object thus yields its fruition as it dilates and divides and merges into the vast range of transitional phenomena (and objects) with which human life is populated. So I put forward the hypothesis that design is also a transitional phenomenon. Winnicott points out that the transitional object is not regressive but progressive, because:

> . . . with its existence it helps the child to grow: seeing that in the course of growth he will be less and less able to keep his mother with him all the time, he will in

exchange be able to keep the blanket for himself [or the teddy-bear and all those objects which are for him a reassuring metaphor for his mother's breast], and as he gradually learns to recognise his existence as separate, he comes to recognise as such that of his mother too.[2]

The second group of thought concerns the reasons why we desire an object: the relationship between function and emotion, and the amusing attempt to utilise the 'Theory of Affective Codes' developed by Franco Fornari (an Italian psychoanalyst) in the language of objects – as indeed we have tried to do in our latest design operation, called Family Follows Function. According to Fornari, two kinds of meaning are constantly present in human language: 'the state of day' (which refers to cognitive data, critical-rational thought and reality, which I would call 'reason/function'), and the 'state of night' (a sort of phylogenetic language common to all men, regardless of their geographic/historical/cultural circumstance, which refers to affective matters and to an oneiric process of communicating and of knowing the world, which I would call 'affections/emotions'). Thus, that part of the mind where desire for an object arises lies in the area of experience situated between dreams and reality (as with Winnicott), between the state of day and the state of night, in other words, in the endless debate which takes place within us whenever we are called upon to make a choice of purchase, and whose process we are never fully conscious of; an endless debate between, precisely, reason/function and affections/emotions.

This second shadowy zone is predominated by fantasy and daydreams. Vigilant thought is temporarily held in check. Criticism and control are reduced, whilst affective representations relating to the symbolic universe of dreams emerge. In following Fornari, I maintain that our own choices are influenced – much more than is commonly supposed – by the structures of symbolic-affective thought (affections/emotions as opposed to reason/function). After analysing my working experience, I have good reasons for thinking that what he called 'Koinems', or primary ideas of life, also decisively guide our subjective, pragmatic choices whenever we find ourselves desiring objects; that these choices are always related to a basic decision-making process which is firmly rooted in our affections. They are unconscious prescriptions to which the affections are bound; a minimal ideogrammatic vocabulary that allows our affections to be transformed into representations, into real things. These 'primary ideas of life' are small in number and simple to define, whereas it is plainly very much more difficult to identify and to catalogue the related representations which they arouse in us. These primary ideas are the 'Erotems', or affective codes allocated to decision-making processes relating to the survival of the species (the code of nudity-erotic corporeity); the 'Parentems', or codes

allocated to decision-making processes relating to the survival of institutions and culture (the maternal/paternal code, the parental code, the child/brothers code), and the 'Koinems of Birth and Death', a universal biological symbolisation of Good and Bad, relating to personal survival (the codes, in fact, of birth and death). Thus, briefly, each object communicates signals to all of us, these signals directly engage our affective codes, and consequently they provoke our reactions, be they negative or positive.

This analysis seems both convincing and clear. On the other hand, the task of coming to a practical definition of the affective structures of the object, of objects, of every object, and also of the practices (and success) of their designers is more difficult. However, as producers we are lucky in that our business brings new cases to our attention all the time, cases represented by the projects we have developed over the years, and urges us to keep the progress of previous cases 'on the market' under observation. By clinically examining these projects a number of interesting examples can be spotted which allow us to take a few steps forward. I should like to mention three such cases drawn from our history.

The first of these is Ettore Sottsass' olive-oil cruets designed in 1978, which in my view clearly exhibit the code of erotic corporeity (something often recalled by the designer himself). After years of observation, I maintain that it is precisely the elegantly phallic shape of his glass cruets which is one of the key elements behind the international success of this design. Another example can be seen in the project for the salt and pepper shakers designed by Pierangelo Caramia in 1991, not to mention the most recent project of Firebird, an electronic gas lighter by Guido Venturini. I don't actually believe it makes sense to feel scandalised: all the history of the Applied Arts, at least since the times of the ancient Egyptian and pre-Columbian cultures is full of examples of the use of this code.

The second example is drawn from the work of Andrea Castiglioni and addresses the importance which he attaches to the 'desire to play'. This is strongly in evidence in a large number of his creations and seems to me to relate to the 'child code'. Thus the gimmick of the balancing lid which opens and closes by itself in his cruets of 1984 (when the cruet is tilted), or still more, the opening-closing component of the edge of his prototype tray of 1982, suggest to me the 'appearing/disappearing' referred to by Baudrillard when he quotes Freud's observations on the 'cotton reel game' and on the tendency to repetition found in traumatic neuroses, in analytical transfers and in particular cases of children's play. A child aged one and a half plays with a wooden cotton-reel and:

    . . . holding the thread to which it was attached, threw . . .
    the reel with great ability out of his bed so as to make it
    disappear, at the same time pronouncing his expressive

'o-o-o-' (= 'away'); then he again was pulling the reel into the bed, and greeted its reappearance with a cheerful 'da' (='here'). This was therefore the complete game – of disappearance and reappearance – the greatest pleasure of which was the undoubtedly derived from the second act. The interpretation of the game became obvious, related to the child's great achievement of civilisation through an impulsive renunciation . . . consisting, without protest, in allowing his mother to go away. The child compensated himself; so to speak, for this sacrifice, by actually putting on the act of disappearing and reappearing . . .

Finally, I come to the work of Philippe Starck. When I think of the repeated use of the horn icon, or of the enigmatic, ambiguous – yet so keenly desired – objects like the Juicy Salif lemon squeezer and the Mr Meumeu cheese dish, it seems to me that the word 'beauty' manifestly fails to describe them, and that the correct term should be sought instead, in the realms of 'perturbation-uneasiness-fear'. His work strikes the inner chords which, in my view, come into connection with the most difficult and dangerous of affective codes. Indeed, Starck seems to me to be an even more daring tightrope-walker, grappling with the great mystery of the affections, and in particular with the 'code of life and death'. I also see part of Andrea Branzi's work in this vein.[3]

Thus, at this point I must admit that Fornari's theory of affective codes can be a useful tool in improving our knowledge of the language of objects. However, it refers only to an initial group of reaction-relations: those that can be retraced to the 'phylogenetic, primary imagination common to all men'. These probably play the most important role in defining the affective structures of objects. But they are not sufficient to explain the intricate system of connections between Man and his things.

To take a further step forward, another set of reaction-relations will have to be examined: that of the historical, ontogenetic, personal memory of individuals, which begins to take shape after the future consumer's first few months of life and ends only with its end. A good example of a design with roots in a child's historical memory is the Girotondo tray, designed in 1989 by Stefano Giovannoni and Guido Venturini. The reasons for its great popularity lie in the decoration of manikins along its edge which at first sight seem too elementary but are actually very meaningful. With this epistemological contribution I felt a little more at ease when I started working on our more recent project called Family Follows Fiction. Following in the footsteps of all those who have worked for thousands of years in the Applied Arts, I know full well that with my work I am answering not so much a primary need (one can turn on and light the gas, boil water, make coffee or tea, add salt and pepper, crack nuts and clean the toilet with far more basic tools than those designed by Alessi) as a desire for happiness felt by people, through the paradoxical dimension of our artifacts.

Attempt at a Conclusion

When we discuss the future of industry I believe that the focal point of the matter is that the whole industrial system is running the risk of making objects which are too ordinary, too boring, without emotions – and this at a time when people, finally free from the hindrances of a conservative culture and from the admonitions of the Modern Movement, have become aware of their wish for art and poetry in all the areas of their lives.

The consequence of the mass production industries acting in this way is that, at a certain point as predicted by the marketing experts, people will become too bored to change their car. And this in spite of the most up-to-date marketing techniques to try to give credibility and justification to products: in the world of communication we have all seen many attempts to find an ingeniously refined remedy for the poorness of the product to be promoted. When I think of how much ability and intelligence is usually spent after the creation process of the product, I feel uneasy: it would be much better if, during the creation process a more important part of this ability, of this ingenuity, were used upriver. In my opinion it is absolutely necessary to turn the process around and to persist in the centrality of the product and the discipline regulating its creation: design.

In that sense, the design factories can be a good example. We don't agree with the role that mass production industry tends to force upon design. We believe that to look at design simply in terms of marketing and technology is too reductive an interpretation. On the contrary, we are convinced that the old time distinction between the Fine Arts and the Minor, Decorative or Applied Arts now constrains design too tightly. And I'm convinced that – as a result of external factors arising from the constant changes in the world around us, and a physiological growth and maturation process of its own – design is now entitled to a kind of historical option: that is to establish its own specific, independent slot within the spectrum of figurative arts.

I would like to insist on another consideration: that design, true design isn't easy to handle. It always provokes a disturbance of habits and certainties in the industrial environment, because it often raises questions and poses problems which in a way unsettle us (at that time busy with more important activities, such as manufacturing, selling, paying, being paid), which seem too difficult, and which the industrial environment cannot answer and solve right away. But these solutions and answers, if we are able to find them, can also improve the general environment, creating a growth which is not only cultural and aesthetic, but also very often technical and of the marketplace as well. In short, results

which are often unforeseeable, unprogrammable and very difficult (so difficult!) to reach by the instruments which the current management techniques put at our disposal, often constitute true design.

Coming to a conclusion, it would be easy to say that the only 'right way' is the way of the design factories, and only this one. Yet since Alessi is one of these factories and I know it well, I can assure you that this kind of industry also has its problems. Thinking about my activity, for example, I would point out that we always tend to work in a natural way, in a zone of people's wishes – and so of the market – which is still unknown. Our mission to explore the *Possibile Creativo* drives us to look for some ways which don't yet exist, to reach people's hearts, to always move on the enigmatic boundary line between what may become real (that is to say objects that are really loved and owned by people) and what will never become real (that is to say objects too far from what, at present, ordinary people are ready to wish and to use). I believe that our Utopia, our vision, risks becoming too virtual, addressing too high and too limited a market, with products which could become progressively too difficult for ordinary people. Products destined only for the design aficionados, the early adopters, the trendy people. And this isn't our goal: our goal is to bring a little more happiness to all people.

But I am also convinced that it is necessary for the industrial culture to recognise and be more aware of the enormous possibilities which the *Possibile Creativo* offers. I believe this is the main point, even if the operative rule system which we use in industry today, which I agree is necessary for the smooth functioning of our industrial organism, leads to a certain severity, an excessive rigidity, in short, an insufficiency in this field.

So what shall we do? I would like to put forward a hypothesis, once again with the help of Franco Fornari's Theory of the Affective Codes. In the last years of his life, Fornari tried to apply this theory, not only to the pathology of people, but also to human organisations. He asserted that at the centre of the balanced functioning of a human group, of all human groups, there is the so-called 'inner good family'. In this inner good family, in order to assure the isomorphism between the unconscious decisional structures of the singles and the surviving of the group, it is necessary to have family codes: in particular the paternal code and the maternal code. According to Fornari, the consumer society is dominated by the imperialism of the child code: with the consumer as omnipotent and privileged child to whom the parents bow with reverence. At the same time he noticed the strong contradiction between the ideological and cultural stereotypes used for production (man who produces is, or is supposed to be, frugal, moderate, laborious, temperate and strong) and for

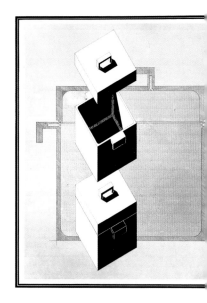

consumption (man who consumes is, on the contrary, greedy, immoderate, leisure-oriented, extravagant and thoughtless).

The organisation of groups, and people, according to Fornari, originates in the division of the codes of the inner family, and in the control of just one of them who turns against the others like a foreign and enemy power. The paternal code, characterised by a desire for the growth, diligence, prestige, social success and also a certain super-ficiality, corresponds to the ideological model of the man who produces. When applied to the case of industry, mass production industry, if this code becomes dominant it may become the imperialistic myth of the technological revolution, with a market geared solely towards business and money.

Opposing this is the maternal code, centred on beauty, lightness, renewal, comprehension and ability to satisfy needs, which in a certain way, is contrary to consumer culture and, allied exclusively to the child code, could cast aside hostility to technology and business, bringing us to live in the Arcadian myth where nature and imagination hold sway.

My hypothesis consists of a continuous research into the balancing of the inner good family even inside the industrial system, and in its relation with society. So at Alessi we have not only one but two general managers, one representing the paternal code and the other the maternal. If we paraphrase we could assert that design factories are closer to the maternal code and mass production industries are closer to the paternal.

We could apply the same criteria to the attention to function, viewing it as a paternal element, and the attention to emotion, as a maternal element. Or again, more generally, European industry (and the European political systems) have some typical maternal characteristics of which they should become more aware as they develop and progres-

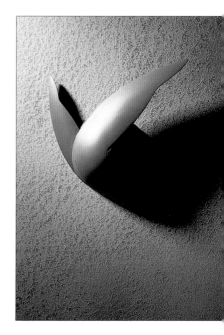

sively change their identity. Here I refer to the orientation towards the Decorative Arts, towards a certain handicraft coming from the centuries-old tradition of our Renaissance workshops, in a word, the orientation towards beauty. This compared to the model of the American and Japanese industry (and their relative political systems), which even if different from each other are more paternal, more centred on mass production, on labour organisation, on performance and on a certain superficiality.

The history of the Applied Arts has been a long one. It has been a journey where real progress has always been looked for by exploring that territory which is situated between the Possible and the Real, between the area of the day and the area of the night. A journey which is still long, and in which the role of industry will be fundamental. I clearly see that the future progress of our society will only be played in a continuous and dynamic dialectic between business and culture.

Meanwhile we continue on our way, even if difficult, complicated and often contradictory. And to advance and continue our Utopia it is necessary that we, as manufacturers of the design factories, make the strongest efforts to preserve, together with the business aspect, another important dimension: the spiritual one (may I say this, being a businessman, a manager who lives thanks to the produc-tion of objects which are, after all, so superficial? Why not!). But this is both for the design factories and mass production industries, there is no difference.

1   DW Winnicott, *Gioco e Tealtà*, Armando, Rome 1990, from the preface by R Gaddini, p11.

2   Ibid.

3   S Freud, *Al di là del principio del piacere*, Tr it 'Opere', vol 9 Boringhieri, Turin 1977, p201 quoted from L Frontori, *Il Mercato dei segni*, Cortina, Milan, 1986, p34.

A BRIEF HISTORY

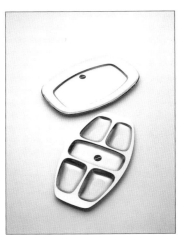

The Twenties

Founded by Giovanni Alessi Anghini in Bagnella di Omegna, the company, in its early days, consisted of a lathe-works factory and foundry. Nickel and brass were worked using strictly artisan production techniques, on commission from external clients. In 1924 for the first time the company began to produce its own trays and coffee makers. Thanks to the introduction of the galvanic bath chroming method, which, together with nickel- and silver-plating, were part of the technical advances of these years, the objects produced were both of a higher quality and more durable. With the FAO trade name (Fratelli Alessi Omegna), the company specialised in this field, though cooking pans and cutlery were not included as they required different technology.

In 1925 the first catalogue was printed, which marked the beginning of direct sales. In 1928, the company moved to Crusinallo.

The Thirties

After studying industrial design in Novara during the first half of the thirties, Carlo (eldest son of Giovanni Alessi) joined the company and began to design: his are the majority of the objects produced from that moment until 1945 (his last project was the 'Bombé' coffee series, still in the catalogue). The company, therefore, began to acquire its own style. It was also a period which marked the beginning of exports to a few European markets, and the experimental working of steel.

The Forties

During the war, with the growing difficulty in gathering materials, the production of household objects almost came to a halt (the production of bowls and carafes in zinc is irrelevant as it proved to be a completely unsuitable material due to its porosity). The company converted to military production: supplying the Army with badges, cannon parts, fuel filters for planes and carburettor floats, on commission from the war industries (Savoia Marchetti in particular).

Ettore, Giovanni's youngest son joined the company in 1945. Keen on mechanics, in a few years he became an expert on the cold pressing of metals. Under his direction, Alessi developed the technical know-how which made it famous and appreciated worldwide. Carlo assumed the responsibility of general manager, abandoning design

activity altogether and, from the fifties, he began to bring outside designers (Mazzeri and Massoni) to Alessi. He launched the company on the international scene thanks to an American commission for brass ladles, which required large investments and a doubling of machinery. From there on the distribution progressively extended to 70 nations.

In 1947 the new trade name Alfra (Alessi Fratelli) replaced FAO, and continued to be used until 1967.

The Fifties

Steel gradually replaced the materials previously used, and the production of chrome- and silver-plated brass objects ended. The company became a joint-stock company and acquired an industrial structure.

It was in 1955 that the collaboration with Massoni and Mazzeri (then Mazzeri and Vitale) began, whose works constitute what today is Programme 4. A few products were selected and presented at the XI Milan Triennale.

The Sixties

The plant in Crusinallo was expanded according to a design by Carlo Mazzeri. During these years the company intensified its presence at all the European exhibitions, appointed an agency for its advertising and, in 1968, with the trade name Ceselleria Alessi created by the Lambert agency to replace Alfra, began its appearances on television advertising.

The Seventies

Alberto (Carlo's eldest son) left the Cattolica University in Milan with a degree in law and began his training at the company involving himself mainly in the commercial side and the communication of the new products. Half way through the eighties he became general manager, responsible for product policies and communication (the other general manager being Michele, his younger brother). The 'Alessi d'après' programme was researched and prepared, in order to create a new dimension to production – being a series of art objects designed by Giò Pomodoro, Carmelo Cappello, Dusan Dzamonja with Pietro Consagra and Andrea Cascella.

The collaboration began with the architects Franco Sargiani and Eija Helander (authors of the company's new graphic image as well as the Programme 8 series), and with Silvio Coppola, Franco Grignani, Pino Tovaglia and Giulio Confalonieri. The plant was extended and the first objects of

the Programme 7 series introduced to the public. In 1972 collaboration with the architect Ettore Sottsass began, mainly concerning the extension of the Programme 5 series.

In 1975, Michele joined the company having obtained a degree in mechanical engineering at Turin's Polytechnic, though he never dealt with technology. Instead, right from the start he dedicated himself principally to organisation and finance, and from the mid-eighties he became general manager in these areas.

Following a development process of five years, Sargiani and Helander's Programme 8 appeared on the market. At the same time the first European level advertising campaign was devised, through Agenzia Italia and the Studio Quadrifoglio in Milan.

In 1977, together with other companies in the furnishing sector, the company became a promoter and publisher of *Modo*, a magazine on design and architecture edited by Alessandro Mendini.

In 1978 collaboration with Richard Sapper began, on the design of Programme 9, and from 1979 Mendini became general design consultant.

The Eighties

This period is characterised by the Programme 6 experiment – the tea and coffee services designed by a group of international architects which concluded in 1983 – and of the birth of the new trade name Officina Alessi, for the research and production of objects which, although originating from the same company, exploited its more artisan oriented side, utilising different metals.

In 1980 Alessio (son of Carlo Alessi), joined the company, and the collaboration with Achille Castiglioni began. Alessio followed a commercial training, and from the mid-eighties became the company's marketing director.

In 1983, under the guidance of Alessandro Mendini with the collaboration of Ettore Sottsass, the renewal of the graphics was finalised: all Alessi production was to be divided between two divisions: 'Alessi' for large-scale production series of general objects in steel; and 'Officina Alessi' for objects in various metals, sometimes of limited production series. In the same year the collaboration with Aldo Rossi began on the large-scale production.

In 1984 Stefano (eldest son of Ettore Alessi), joined the company and the collaboration with Michael Graves began on the large-scale production. Stefano followed a technical training and today is director of purchasing.

In 1986 collaboration with Philippe Starck started, with the first objects appearing in 1990.

In 1987 the large typological and materials diversification began to take place, with the first catalogue of watches, followed by the series of objects in wood (1988) under the Twergi label, the first catalogue of small furnishings (1989), and the first catalogue of ceramic objects under the Tendentse label (1990).

The Nineties

In January 1990 the Centro Studi Alessi opened in Milan, with the double objective of developing contributions on design and object theory, and of co-ordinating the work of young designers.

RIGHT FROM ABOVE: Oval holder, lid and oven-to-table glass dish, Sergio Asti, 1983; 'Mizhar' trays, Paola Navone, 1984; 'Nuovo Milano' cutlery service, Ettore Sottsass, 1989; Press filter coffee makers, mug and cups, Aldo Rossi, 1991; 'Simona' vase, Simon Dreyfuss, 1989; BELOW: Alessi factory, Crusinallo; PAGE 16 BACKGROUND: Manufacturing process; INSET FROM ABOVE L TO R: Round wire basket (Ufficio Tecnico Alessi); citrus fruit basket, 1952 (Ufficio Tecnico Alessi); soup tureens, 1964 (Ufficio Tecnico Alessi); 'Avio' coffee set, Carlo Mazzeri and Anselmo Vitale, 1961; PAGE 17 FROM ABOVE: The manufacture of trays from Programme 3; cocktail shaker 870, Luigi Massoni and Carlo Mazzeri; 'Dani' tea and coffee services and series 101, 1956 and 1963 (Ufficio Tecnico Alessi); 'Avio' trays, Carlo Mazzeri and Anselmo Vitale, 1961; 'Square', Silvio Coppola, 1977

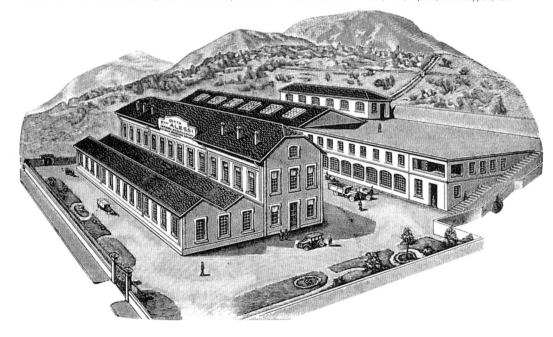

PROGRAMME 8
A SYSTEMATIC RENEWAL OF HOUSEHOLD GOODS FROM 1970

 Programme 8 is a vast and complex design project that has progressively developed into a system of objects structured according to diverse typologies. In 1970, Franco Sargiani and Eija Helander, a Finnish architect, were asked to design an oil jug which later prompted a revised study of tableware objects. During the course of seven years, their global project led to the creation of many trays and food containers on a scale never before attempted. Sargiani and Helander sought primarily to design objects that satisfied functional requirements: the objects should be of maximum adaptability and flexibility, they should enhance the foods without detracting visibly from them, and they should be capable of using space more efficiently.

The hypothesis of creating a system of tableware which redefined behavioural patterns fascinated the company: it would replace all the traditions associated with the history of food and the containers that hold it. The choice of steel was perfect for this task. The premise was that steel should be used for its own qualities and not as a substitute for more precious metals, which would allow steel to acquire its own particular identity.

The programme that Sargiani and Helander proposed represented a radical change of direction for a company tied to the process of embossing, which traditionally aimed at exclusive sectors of the market with specific products. This programme was to exclude the elitist choice and target the far larger market of modern professionals.

This new emerging class (with no correlation to the traditional system of social classes) needed useful, practical objects without any 'formal recipe', as Sargiani affirms. A prevalently young consumer market residing in cramped living spaces became the new behavioural models of society, capable of modifying the habits and rules for eating.

The most important phase in the project was the research programme: at first Sargiani and Helander conducted an extensive survey of the measurements and capacities of foreign and Italian tableware objects. By analysing and defining the various functions of tableware, they identified two target groups: the principals and the accessories. The first (trays and containers) are for general everyday use, and

the second for a more specific market. From the studies carried out on the characteristics of foods in international cooking, the commonly used quantities and methods, Sargiani and Helander identified a series of measurements (both in size and weight) to establish a modular dimensional grid to determine the shape of future objects.

At this point the square and rectangular forms of the pieces seemed to be an inevitable choice for easy storage. It seemed obvious that rounded forms would not be used as they excluded aggregation and amplification. Yet transforming such objects from round to square on the basis of mathematics and geometry ignored the tradition of familiar household objects.

The 'ritual' of seeing food surrounded by the edge of the dish is a difficult memory to remove. The different psychological effects produced by food on a round porcelain plate or in a square steel bowl are such that they can affect the taste – though at the same time there was no way of evaluating the psychological effect that this transformation might bring about.

In making the bowls and modular containers square, there was a technological difficulty: the steel is weakened through the tensions along the sides and the corners, a difficulty which could only be overcome by not considering the cost and ironically reconfirming the belief of the company's technicians that the 'square shape of the design for steel products is perhaps unnatural!' But the combination of trays and containers was realised exactly as planned, and like a never ending spiral, the designed pieces multiplied, reaching ever more specialist definitions.

Programme 8 is a famous product for Alessi, copied all over the world. It was loved and shunned by the public and the critics alike. The company found it difficult to maintain the initial success of the product with a public who found the system fascinating but was often perplexed and incapable of using it. Now, almost two decades on from its presentation, the overconfident intention to be 'the' new system of household goods has been abandoned. Nowadays, Programme 8 tends to be restricted in its distribution network. Ironically the typologies and elements which it has created have become restricting rather than liberating, and Programme 8 has become the antithesis of its original intention.

RIGHT FROM ABOVE: Permutations of Programme 8

GALASSIA   ALESSI — MENDINI

CATALOGHI   BOMBÉ
STORIA
PAESAGGIO CASALINGO
LIBRO
TIGER   SISTEMATICA
MOSCONI
CONICA ROSSI
1978   TRIENNALE
HOLLEIN
VENTURI
LIBRO   GRAVES
TUSQUET
THE AND COFFE PIAZZA   DECORO-   LIBRO
NAVONE
MEYER   CIBI E RITI   BERLINO
CAFFETTIERA NAPOLETANA   RICCARDO
LIBRO
CINTURA DI ORIONE   SAPPER   STARCK   OFFICINA
NOUVEL
DESIGN FRANCESE   SOLFERINO   NEMO
POZAMPARK
LIBRO ALBERTO
NOT IN PROD-   LIBRO SCARZELLA
NEXT TO PROD-

KING KONG   PAESAGGIO DA CUCINA CON PENTOLE
SOLOVIEW
ASPEN   ISOZAKI   GIOCO
DEI POMOLI
PENTOLE FALSTAF
COMPLEMENTI
CUCINA   DI ARREDO
FORNETTO   MARI
BONET
LAGO ORTA   CASA FELICITA   CASTIGLIONI
ROSSI
NUOVO STAND 1989   PASSERO SOLITARIO   SOTTSASS
PROFUMO   RAMS
SAX   GALASSIA
LEGNO TORNITO
TWERGI   VETRO....
CERAMICA   CRISTALLO...
TENDENTZE   1990

ALESSI 20

THE METAPROJECT

The metaproject is the name given to the generation of design ideas, as realised in the projects produced by Alessi since 1970. In certain aspects it is similar to Marcel Duchamp's approach in the field of figurative arts in the twenties, where an ordinary element of existence was placed in such a way as to allow conventional functioning to disappear thus creating a new ideology for the object. This development of the design idea affords greater artistic expression, allowing objects to be re-evaluated and redesigned under the terms of semiological exploration, rather than being bound by the normal guidelines of the established design process.

Working within the metaproject transcends the creation of an object purely to satisfy function and necessity. Each object represents a tendency, a proposal and an indication of progress which has a more cultural resonance.

This freedom in research allows each project and therefore each object to be more flexible, capable of renewing and changing in such a way as to allow for technical competence, artistic quality and the exploration of a tactile, aesthetic and sensual perception.

Different types of research can be initiated together, of which some can be developed and others will be abandoned. Some can later be reapplied to another aspect of the metaproject while other research programmes will be transformed into something completely different. Certain projects do not give definitive results or products, but generate a rich experience of planning ideas that will subsequently create other products. Every research programme opens a new direction, an array of possibilities, a land to explore from an expressive cultural and techno-

logical point of view, in order to obtain success.

The amount of prototypes built are proof of the range of experiments; the potential that is represented by the metaproject, where the object is no longer the end product but its implications and the developmental route are more important. At the same time every designer has the opportunity to experiment, verifying the limits of their work by applying the constraints of technology. This, therefore, becomes an exceptional situation and at the same time part of the global metaproject discourse by Alessi.

The metaproject is a complex retainer of information, inferences and suggestions intended for the creation of objects and a far larger project. Therefore in the metaproject the possibilities of producing something new and diverse are ample. But for this to come about it is necessary to project-plan at all levels: both the designer and even the industrialist have to project-plan. The industrialist also has to modify himself, he has to become a mediator, the director who continually provides stimulation and space for the designer, designers whom he may choose for their methods of metaproject planning, to coagulate the industry's image with certain basic ideas. The ideas of the collaborators are organised and realised following a philosophy that unhinges the mathematical insensibility of industrial logic. Industry becomes a workshop where people work next to each other, exchanging their ideas and opinions, suggesting new ideas, defining production with a constant control of practices.

The metaproject is therefore an amalgamation of many research programmes that have and are evolving and progressing inside the Alessi workshops. This is how the products from the Alessi workshop come about.

RIGHT FROM ABOVE: 'Falstaf' saucepans, Alessandro Mendini, 1989; Aldo Rossi wearing his 'Momento' watch, 1987; wooden napkin rings, Ettore Sottsass, 1994 (Twergi); OPPOSITE: Alessandro Mendini's illustration of the Alessi Galaxy

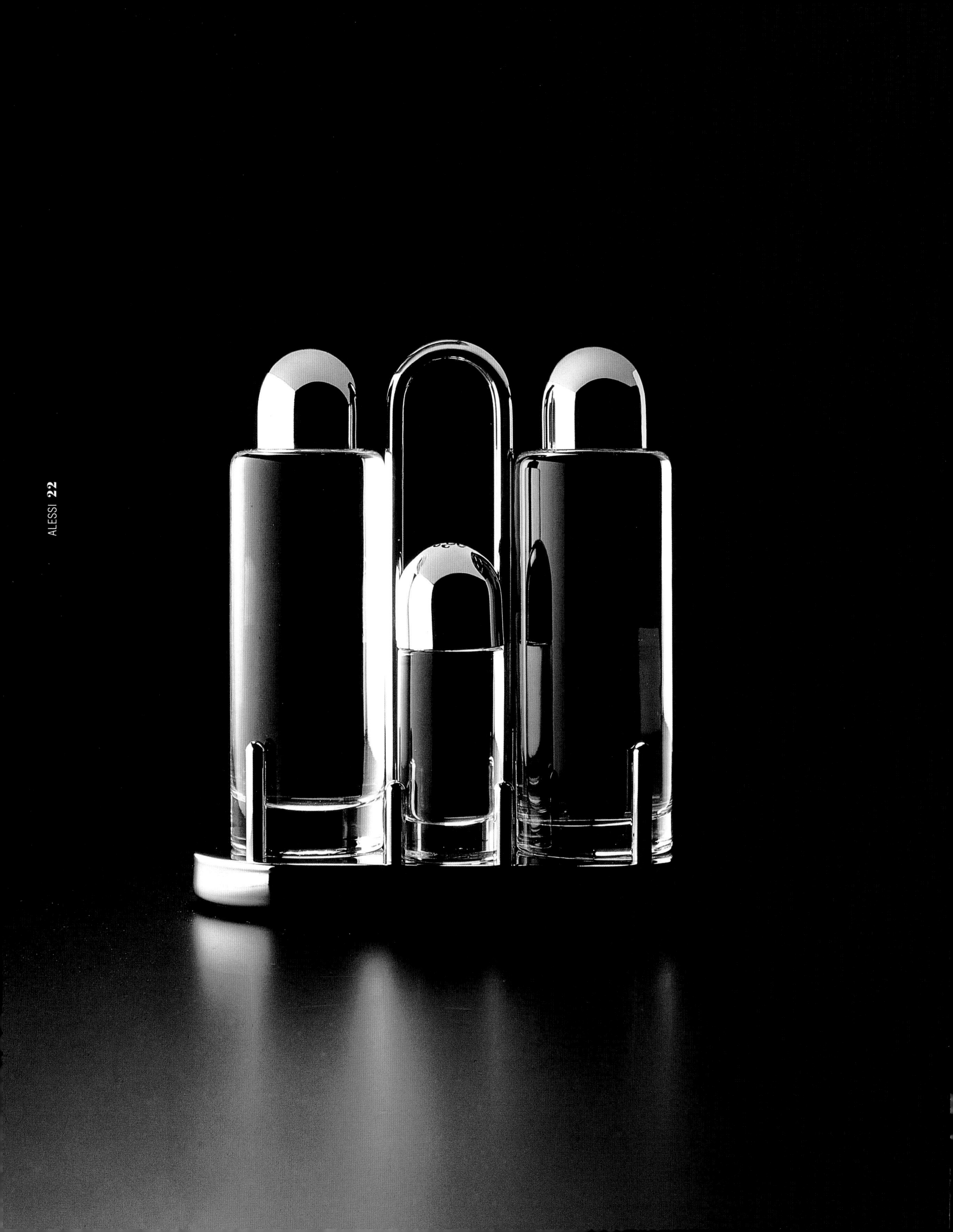

ETTORE SOTTSASS

The contacts with Ettore Sottsass began parallel to the collaboration with Silvio Coppola and Co. Franco Sargiani[1] brought him to me at Crusinallo in 1972. I met him together with uncle Ettore, and he made a great impression on me. He was the first figure of really international stature whom I had dealt with, and he arrived at Alessi preceded by the fame of his work at Olivetti, the 'Valentine' typewriter in particular, as well as his reputation as radical design guru.

Ettore was immediately interested in our themes, and began to design some trays (the records of which, unfortunately, have been lost from our archives) which were swollen with large borders, as was his style in those days. We quickly decided that that was not the right direction, and we asked him to apply himself to the theme of oil cruets. Together with his assistant, the Finnish Ulla Salovaara, he quickly designed a group of objects that we were quite pleased with, but which presented great technical manufacturing difficulties: the crystal containers for the oil and vinegar were secured to the tray by small steel rods inserted beneath them through a hole, and our crystal supplier judged the thing impossible to manufacture. Between one discussion and the next, we dragged the project on for a few years until Michele, who had recently joined, took an interest in it. Since he was involved, amongst other things, with technology and suppliers, he offered to carry it forward on his own initiative, firmly reopening the dialogue with the supplier, and allowing us to bring it successfully to completion, launching it on the market in 1978.

The success of the 5070 has been a rolling and continuous one. It is probably one of the best projects developed by us in the last twenty years (the most archetypal), one of the few objects in continual – although measured – quantitative growth since I've been involved with product policy. The reason certainly lies in the exceptional global appeal of this product: its very pleasant form, good functional design, and justified price – although high . . . all of this summarised in a typology that constitutes the most difficult theme to be offered to a designer within our sector. No wonder there aren't any oil cruets on the market which even come close to these very successful objects (which then in a certain sense don't have any competition).

Speaking of Ettore, I can't help thinking of his considerable charm, he's a sort of philosopher able to say interesting things about any subject, and he has had a considerable influence on me. It was with him that I began to discuss the important themes in design and the role of industry. He told me one day:

You industrialists, whether you know it or not, are forever assuming a very important cultural role: for the simple reason that you produce and distribute millions, tens of millions, billions of objects destined to influence people's lives, therefore the culture of the society in which we live . . .

And I won't forget that.

In 1978 I suggested to him that we should publish a book on his designs. I actually meant working designs, I was thinking about a series of those nice sketches of his to document the succession of his projects with us. Instead he drew and wrote *Esercizio formale* (*Formal exercise*), a sort of memoir of travels/meditations, composed during a navigation of the Greek Islands, which we launched in November 1979 at the Studio Marconi, attended by many architects, designers and related people.

Ettore remains the designer with the largest number of objects in our catalogues (even in those of Twergi and Tendentse), and with Sottsass Associati he is also responsible for a great part of our graphics. At 77 years old, he has exceptional physical, mental and creative strength, and I'm sure that even the new projects on which he is working for us at the moment (a Pyrex holder, a thermal jug, a range of baskets and table glasses: the first Alessi glasses!) will be of very high quality and will be welcomed by the public.

Even though – due to a certain reluctance on my behalf, as if I am afraid to erode my relationship with him – we frequent each other rather sporadically, though always with great reciprocal pleasure, he was the first figure I met through work to become a real mentor to me: of life and beliefs, as they used to say.

His wish, together with Alessi, is to assemble, in time, a complete collection of objects for the table and the kitchen, referring specifically to his fellow countryman Joseph Hoffman's precedent with The Wiener Werkstätte at the beginning of the century. I hope we'll succeed.

Extract Alberto Alessi's Factory Journal

1 Young Milanese architect, art director at Alessi in the early 1970s.

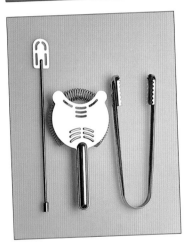

The Boston Shaker and Bar Accessories, 1979

The tall cooling buckets, the Boston shakers and bar accessories, designed by Sottsass in consultation with Alberto Gozzi, are some of the most advanced examples of the formal evolution of these typologies.

Because of the golden rules of serving cool wine and champagne, the cooling buckets come in two sizes easily adaptable to the bottles they need to hold. One of the sizes is ideal for the tall, thin wine bottles that come from the Rhine, while the other size is much lower and larger for the Bordeaux, Burgundy and Champagne bottles. Their construction is quite specific because of the important functional requirements: for example, the body is made of a different thickness of steel. A specific lathe, called a *répoussage*, shapes the bucket's sides to a certain thickness by thinning out and stretching the metal to eventually form the edges and the bottom, making them heavier than the rest of the object. This process strengthens the bucket by hardening the sheet metal and allowing the steel to become temperate. The bucket's edge is totally turned around itself, making it much stronger and easier to handle. The handles have been designed to a size that makes them easy to grasp, even with just one hand, as a professional would use them. The handles are the most formal detail, and were the most problemmatic in their design, though eventually a solution was found. They are hollow, making them easier to solder to the body of the cooler, and closed at the ends with a pressurised coloured metal cap. Originally they were conceived as rectangular, but research showed this to be an extremely expensive if technically possible option. The knob, with the same technical characteristics, is round in shape with a flat bottom part, allowing the buckets to be easily stacked one on top of the other. This component requires the most complex production process, with ten different operations compared to the few production phases to make the body.

The bucket stand is a sophisticated piece of service equipment designed to take up less space on the table. It is made in three different sections (the base, the pole and the supporting top) and is easily dismantled, making it easy to store or deliver. Even the dimensions and formal details depend a lot on its use and requirements. The supporting top is 60 centimetres high, easily reached by whoever is serving or eating and is designed to keep the bucket from becoming tarnished or scratched. There is a surrounding well to retain any water leaking down from the bucket, and the supporting stand's handles are quite prominent to allow easy transportation.

The Boston shaker is very fifties in style, and, according to a publicity campaign by Emanuele Pirella and Michele Goetsche, is 'the rebirth of the shaker as it once was, when it was invented on a boat that cruised up and down the Mississippi.' The shaker consists of two equal parts – one of steel and the other of glass – that are slotted into each other, serving not only as a shaker but also as a mixing glass. The stirrer that used to be inside the traditional-style shakers made in three parts, has now become a separate accessory.

In designing such a specific product as the shaker, it is important to remember the strong bond that exists with tradition when using a shaker, as well as its functional requirements.

These – say Alberto Gozzi – can be determined when the new product becomes accepted. At the end of the day it is the professional use that will determine its success.

The Serving Dish with a Bell-shaped Cover, 1983

The serving dish with a bell-shaped cover to keep food hot, originated in the eighteenth-century. It was an object created especially for silver and represents an aristocratic concept, used both for serving and as a display piece on the table. Today steel has almost completely replaced silver in the manufacture of this item which now tends to be technically quite simple, and produced in similar versions by many companies. The formal aspects necessitated by its uses seem almost untouchable, with the exception of a few indistinguishable detailed features that often escape the eyes of the non-expert.

Here the objective was to create a plate in stainless steel, sophisticated enough to replace the silver versions in high class hotels. Alberto Gozzi studied the functional necessities, allowing Sottsass to respond with plans and designs. He discovered that the bell-shaped cover needed to be light, robust, and easy to position on the specified part of the serving plate, unlike other versions on the market which were unstable on the plates. It would need to be easily cleaned, especially at the sides which would have to be without angles. For hygienic reasons, the sides in particular required careful consideration for hotel usage: strict American health regulations stipulated that they would have to be smoothly curved or even wide curved in order to facilitate thorough cleaning.

Sottsass formally maintained the detail of the sides' curvature which proved to be an important feature in the commercial success of the product. It has become very popular with its elegant refinements, making it a worthy successor to its silver predecessors.

An important feature is the ease with which the dish can be stacked, something facilitated by the covers' curvature and the handle which is set into the cover. (Amongst the many projects developed by Sottsass in reaching the final cover, a piece that the company considered very interesting was omitted because of its inability to be stacked, its beautiful bell-shaped curvature was too prominent and thus prevented the easy stacking of other dishes on top.) Alberto

Gozzi said that it's success with the public depended upon it: fitting in well with the traditional range of things already seen but with particular technical characteristics. Utility, tradition and design are this time all in harmony with each other.

I began working with Alessi, or Alberto Alessi to be exact, about 25 years ago. That was a long time ago. Alberto Alessi was very young, and I was about fifty. Both of us were curious, very curious indeed: Alberto was curious to see how he could become an industrialist who was not only aware of his monetary destiny, but also of that other unique destiny in which any event (even an industrial event) may sometimes take its place in history by offering something to history, that is to say, the more or less sophisticated, profound and ambiguous history of interpretations of our restless existence.

I, too, was in more or less the same position, and I was (and still am) extremely curious to see what I might contribute to the interpretation or description or design of a metaphor of existence which, as we all know, is in constant motion . . . Because of all this, we soon became friends, and our relationship became that of curious friends, of friends who discuss things, and friends who know how fragile obscure,

and ambiguous their plan to lay traps for history may be, but who at least to stick with these plans and do not give in to the constant pull of our changing existence.
We made many plans together, many designs – as we say – for products, and we always intended (even Alberto's decision to search me out reflects this) to design products which, in the end, would leave space for the greatest existential freedom, that freedom left to a hammer, to pincers and to a comb, and (perhaps) even to a bottle, a light-bulb and all those tools our existence needs to carry on, not only to take shape or rather, shall we say, to take shape starting almost from scratch. In other words, we thought we could design products that were tools for existence rather than tools for the sake of being.
Perhaps these tools for the sake of being are designed by poets, philosophers or maybe even great mathematicians: unique, truly unique individuals.
In any case my work with Alberto Alessi, and now with his brothers and their colleagues, is truly a pleasure; we understand each other perfectly, we all have more or less the same obsessions, the same moral outlook and even the same uncertainties, which are dissolved during meetings through patient glances and cryptic smiles.
Ettore Sottsass, November 1993

RIGHT FROM ABOVE: covered dishes and platters, 1983; round pierced basket and oven-to-table glass dish, 1981; Hors-d'oeuvre set, 1982; rectangular tray and round tray with engraving, 1982; OPPOSITE FROM ABOVE: full product range – Boston shaker and accessories, wine coolers and stand and bar accessories, 1979; PAGE 22: Condiment set with oil, vinegar, salt and pepper holders, 1978; PAGE 23 FROM ABOVE: condiment set; full product range including parmesan cheese cellar

16/3/78

RICHARD SAPPER

Richard made his entrance in Crusinallo on Shrove Tuesday, 1977. Dad, Uncle Ettore and myself gathered to welcome him. He was dressed all in black, with a funny black pointed hat. We immediately got on well with each other. Sapper has designed a few historic projects for us – not only as far design culture is concerned but also for the economic history of Alessi – veritable 'line' and 'approach' firsts, 'eighties icons', including the 9090 Cafetiere (the object to which I'm most inexorably linked, I think: it was the first Alessi object for the kitchen since the time of Grandfather Giovanni, our first cafetiere and the first 'amphibious object'), and the 9091 Kettle (the first of the 'designer kettles' and the first 'kitchen decor' object).

Since the cutlery project wasn't making progress, I obtained permission from the 'elders' to attempt an unprecedented step, to enter an area of the home which we had kept deliberately clear of since grandfather's times: the kitchen. [Alessi had initially contacted Sapper on the advice of Sottsass to work on the design of a cutlery service for Programme 8.] The reason for this reticence was historical and very simple: we had developed through the course of the years a type of production organisation which, although much less complex than today's, was still oriented (as it is today) towards a kind of 'mechanised craftsmanship' rather than large-scale series production, to which, on the other hand, two other popular homeware companies in Omegna, Lagostina (saucepans) and Bialetti (espresso cafetieres) had devoted themselves. In fact these mass production companies were typical producers of kitchen implements of satisfactory quality and low cost, and for reasons of closeness, of friendship and of human respect, we had progressively confined ourselves to the area of homeware accessories. We believed that in that area of production our quality and our prices had better chances of being accepted by the market.

Sapper's espresso cafetiere, the 9090 (1977-79), was for me the first textbook example of a very professional approach to product policy: conscious of ground level problems, I had the intuition that the kitchen could be a good area for our enterprises (indeed during the course of the eighties the kitchen substantially changed its sociological status, becoming 'the receptacle of domestic imagery'). I understood that there was a market for a cafetiere totally different from the others, even if a lot more expensive, and

also that this was a more technically complex theme than our usual ones. I realised that we needed a designer with a very highly inventive capacity together with a technological sensitivity.

According to market research, the Italian market for espresso cafetieres was stable around five million pieces per year, of which over two thirds were aluminium and dominated, naturally, by the Bialetti 'Moka' of grandfather Alfonso. All the models were of extremely low cost, even the steel ones. I had convinced myself that our cafetiere, produced at the top of Alessi's state of the art, would be distributed at around double the cost of the most expensive one in existence, and with great courage and intuition I set myself a target of two per cent of the market: 100,000 pieces.

Sapper, probably, really was the most suitable person for the job, and gladly accepted the task, but for some time he engaged in technological audacities, like the fastening without a rubber seal, and the top receptacle in Pyrex glass, which pissed off Uncle Ettore (I remember that whilst with this project Dad stopped keeping a close eye on me in product policy, Uncle would be breathing down my neck for a long time yet, at least until the mid-eighties). Actually, at some point Uncle lost interest in the project and the designer, and left me to handle the hot potato with Prina and Casalino, our two chief technicians, limiting himself to throwing in our direction from time to time, one of those fearsome (sometimes paralysing for me) grimaces of his.

As if by a miracle, and with a great deal of suffering on my behalf – because I usually considered myself to be a victim, the only standard bearer of an experimentation for which I felt destined to be the only one responsible if anything went wrong, while having to share with everybody else the eventual success – after little more than a year the prototype was ready, and Sapper brought it along to Crusinallo, unable to hide his excitement as he pulled it out of his case.

It really was a revolutionary cafetiere, in practice it didn't have a neck or a spout, it looked like a rocket. I myself was a little surprised and a little hesitant: I had to hold it in front of me for quite a while to be able to understand it. It was, in other words, a really innovative project for its type, which surprised me and made me make an effort to make it mine. As I often do today, I showed it to a lot of people, to check their reactions. For example, I showed it to Mendini who was enthusiastic, a reaction which was very comforting. In 1979, the year of its introduction, we sold 110,000 pieces of the

ACHILLE CASTIGLIONI

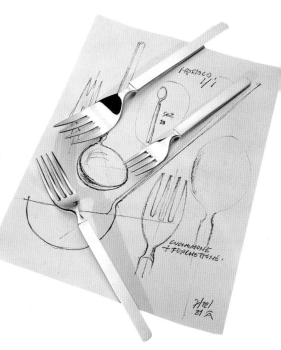

[Achille Castiglioni first worked with Alessi, on Mendini's suggestion, on the design of the two exhibitions at the Design Forum in Linz (1980) and the International Design Centre in Berlin (1981).] The first meeting with Achille Castiglioni, 'the laughing designer', took place in his studio in Piazza Castello in Milan, where he had placed in the entrance a great wall mirror that reflected the interior of his office, so that people used to move towards the mirror to greet him confusing him with his reflected image. I was returning from the Triennale exhibition, and I was very curious to meet one of the legendary figures of Italian design.

Those were two clear and simple installations [the exhibitions], worthy of the best Castiglioni. Naturally we were curious about each other, and after a few talks we found a possible subject for design in a cutlery series. From his precious archives he pulled out a few sketches, prototypes and designs developed in the fifties with his brother Pier Giacomo. They served as the inspiration and starting point for the 'Dry' service, our first cutlery service (1981-84). A great success, despite the marketing people's initial lack of confidence ('You can't present yourselves on the market and expect to sell only one model of cutlery: it is imperative to have a complete range!'), and the decidedly high cost. With 'Dry', we began an extremely successful venture in that sub-area, typical of our sector, but up until then a stranger to Alessi's production traditions. We presented ourselves as complete outsiders with new and interesting models, not only as far as the form was concerned but also because they were all characterised by a great complexity of execution and by price bands where no other international manufacturer had ventured before (perhaps with the only exception of Rosenthal).

I discovered that our retailers also love dealing with cutlery, because they occupy little room in relation to their value and establish a faithful clientele, because in time pieces get lost and it becomes necessary to replace them.

In his work, Castiglioni is fond of – shall we say – 'un-trendy' subjects, where there must be a 'spark', which can be provoked by an innovation or a functional idea. It is difficult to get him to work if this 'spark' isn't there. He has great admiration for 'anonymous design', and has a formidable collection crammed in a cabinet in his office, gathered personally, or through friends from every part of the world. He uses these pieces at conferences, which have a great

following and are admired because of his extraordinary powers of communication and gestural verve (even if he only speaks Italian, he is very much in demand abroad).

I consider Castiglioni to be a great master, curious about everything, and with a great gift for irony and exceptional modesty, but able to design masterpieces. He is very realistic, 'Milanese style', and understands the public well ('cinc ghèi pussè, ma luster' he used to say about the preference of our public for polished finishes).

His practices involve a high degree of interest in the theme being dealt with, he is incapable of applying himself to any kind of request he's not interested in, and he doesn't like a brief that's too constricting. His 'Phil' cruets (1982) and the 7617 Tray (1983), greatly insisted upon by me and which I followed with great passion for years because I considered them to be two extremely important projects, didn't enjoy great success. It is clear that it is better to leave him to work on deeply felt themes (like many of his colleagues, for that matter). He values the maximum degree of human and direct rapport with the commissioner, and the only way to get him to work is to make him enjoy himself, in other words, presenting him with an fun idea for a project. The best ideas came to us in front of a glass of whisky.
Extract Alberto Alessi's Factory Journal

The Condiment Set 1980-84

The main technical feature of these oil and vinegar cruets are their self-raising lids, operated by a counterweight on the outside which causes the top to spring open when the cruet is tipped for pouring. A small, clever invention, fun to use and at the same time very practical, the oil cruet, charged with an expressive quality all its own, is both gay and ironic, two parameters close to the designer's heart.

'The trouble with oil and vinegar cruets', explains Achille Castiglioni, 'is the lid: when you take it off you never know what to do with it. It's always hanging around'. The lid attached to the cruet by a counterweight brilliantly solves the problem, adding an element of pleasure:

awareness of the designer's enjoyment in devising the object gives enjoyment to the user. I believe this is the kind of satisfaction we should look for in artificial objects for common use, a proper way of understanding them.

The unusual shape of the glass receptacle, a line devised to enable the straight handle to be easily clasped, is also both practical and amusing, as is the handle designed as a

T-section, typical of iron. The result is a distinctive *objet à la* Castiglioni, in which ornament is never an end in itself but the expression of a well-defined, poetic and original mode of use.

The oil and vinegar cruets, both different in size, and each with its own drip-catcher base, can be used independently without moving the entire set. A small rimless, grooved tray stays on the table as a support for the cruets. Finally, to stop once and for all asking: 'please pass the salt', a small personal crystal salt shaker completes this anomalous set of single components.   *Patrizia Scarzella*

Before I talk about my relationship with Alessi, the company, I must first explain my personal relationship with Alberto, the entrepreneur.

Naturally, Alessi's design concept is so broad that there was just the right space and positioning for my own design concept. And I feel great in this space . . . This element of enjoyment is an integral part of both my own and Alessi's designs. I feel that our willingness to enjoy our work is ultimately an attempt to communicate with others, however great or small their numbers. The quality of a design lies in the ability to clearly communicate the object's true identity . . .

The anthropological proof of my design is rather important if I want to avoid working merely to satisfy the market . . . The fundamental connection, therefore, is the continuous confrontation between the variability of various design processes.

I agree with Alessi when he states that design is a Global Creative Discipline with an exquisitely artistic and poetic base, and not simply one of the many tools used by marketing and technology to improve sales and production. Alberto Alessi, in my opinion is neither timid nor green around the edges as he seems, even if he is truly young at heart. He is clearly today's brightest and bravest entrepreneur, unhindered by preconceived notions.

I believe that the qualities that draw me towards Alberto Alessi's work are his experiments in that relational space where the objects used create a close bond of both curiosity and devotion between the designer and the user, ultimately leading to a cordial pleasure in even the most simple and humble functions.   Achille Castiglioni, September 1993

RIGHT FROM ABOVE L TO R: Full product range of 'Phil', 1982; 'Spirale', ash tray with spiral, 1970; rectangular tray with handles, 1983; storage box for 'Dry' cutlery (not in production); OPPOSITE: The condiment set; PAGE 30: Achille Castiglioni with 'Dry' cutlery; PAGE 31: 'Dry' with initial sketches

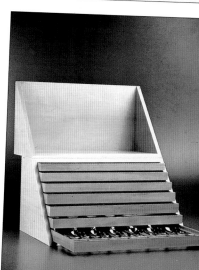

ALESSANDRO MENDINI

My Rapport with Alberto Alessi

I've been collaborating with Alberto Alessi, who has been my main interlocutor within his company, for many years. Our working method is very simple: a continuous sequence, albeit not very frequent, of conversations, reasoning and general ideas, that gradually focus themselves in projects, contacts, objects and exhibitions. Alberto, as far as designers are concerned, is the ideal industrialist, the perfect provocateur. Thus, through the years, our reciprocal professional esteem has developed into a personal friendship, which has brought us to the rare experience of his project, the Casa della Felicità (or 'house of happiness'). This is more than a design for a house, for me it was a deep psychological research, as well as being the theoretical background for all Alessi's experimental production. Amongst the many design directions with which the firm is addressing the nineties – after going through the eighties – Alberto represents the charismatic element, the undisputed ingenious and cultural presence. The results of the enterprise are the fruition of the structured synthesis of the two cores: first, the demand for objectivity and tradition inherent in the history of the enterprise itself, so strong and demanding that it amalgamates with the second, the intuitions of Alberto, who, in the internal dialectics of Alessi, represents the subjective pole, the dreamer of happy seasons, of social Utopias and of enchanted objects. I have to say that this precise, ingenious, shy, gentle person has given me some of the best opportunities within my job as designer, but it also has to be said that all the Alessis, father and brothers, are 'full of history', of the noble class of Italian design.

Alessandro Mendini, December 1993

The Progress of Alessi

I'd like to illustrate here the means by which the Alessi company entered the nineties, with an extremely complex 'magma', subject to constant adjustments, variations and innovations. It was the book Domestic Landscape *that initiated the company's process of self-awareness, which, with a growth initially not systematic, had accumulated a vast number of objects, some of which were extremely*

brilliant and successful. That study laid the foundations for a radical transformation. Its contents schematised the principal expansion policies, forecast an editorial activity, set the initial operations which opened themselves up to a vast selection of new collaborators and put Alessi on the cultural map of design of the Second Modernism. The seventies saw the company install itself on the institutional scene of the Italian bel design *with great prestige but without being perturbed by the more subtle experiences of radical design. In fact, three goals were pursued: firstly, an authoritative examination (as guiding light) of the history of the household object, not only within the meaning of the designer-object, but also within the wider scope of materialistic culture; secondly, an experimental formulation of the Alessi company model in the post-industrial productive culture, with aesthetic, as well as economic, ends; and finally, the creation of an 'Alessi Style' which through a language phenomenon would create compact and recognisable families of 'exemplary' objects. The basic philosophy is, still now, not to point directly to the design of new objects, but rather to the creation of indirect 'thematic spheres', of nebulas of a wide cultural breadth which, through the progressive focusing of their parts and sub-parts, are able to render, as a possible but not definite result, even catalogue objects (if this method hadn't been used the main best-sellers wouldn't exist today). Thus today there are various, and sometimes risky, paths to follow: the institution of a workshop systematically expanding on research, prototypes and trials; or the jump towards the silver chisel, towards new materials, towards a museum of domestic-wares, towards a school of restoration, just as, at least on a theoretical level, there was the architectural experience with* La Casa della Felicità. *Having started from the particular of the household object, Alessi expressed the necessity of reversing the point of view: the themes had to be extended to encompass everything, including the landscape of the habitat. In this way, industry bases its ideology on the absolute matching of the object intended as functional instrument and the same object in its quality of emitter of messages, of spiritual holder of tales to be told. The eighties has been a decade of great interest: the problems upon* which much attention was focused were those of Postmodernism (which leaves a deep trace on the methodologies), and the approach towards young languages, of a playful and oneiric quality. When I examine Alessi's operations with this interpretative key, I'm of the opinion that Alessi's answer to these problems was far-sighted, and skirted the transitoriness of time, retaining the most worthy elements and avoiding the decadence that often marked the decade. Today we strive towards a kind of wide ranging super-functionalism, involving symbols, yearnings and ancestral customs, the flat crudeness of modern living steered towards the formulation of a contemporary mythology. Hence, the Alessi object of the nineties wants to be exemplary: an affectionate companion, extracting from the fragmented elements of the contemporary world some notions of life lived as a sentiment. And to think that today 'friendly objects' can exist around the home, an industrial subspecies, and that such objects are becoming typical and representative forms of contemporary visual art, at a time when other art forms are declining. Thus the Alessi object is defined today as an aesthetic and affective interlocutor, as can be seen in the succession of the various experiences of the Study Centre directed by Laura Polinoro. The idea of liberating Alessi from the conditioning of 'home-wares only' and 'steel only' is not a recent one. The diversification became practicable from the moment the word 'Alessi' didn't coincide any longer with its initial products, but represented an image associated with objects of any kind, assured, guaranteed and culturally progressive. Alessi elaborates these problems through a galactic vision of them as a whole: whilst controlling and optimising the dimension of the parent company it creates an ensemble of brands and of other small independent companies, each and every one responding to their own internal logic within the context of general laws (Twergi, Alessofono, Tendentse . . .). This is very different from putting artisanship into reverse gear. Rather, it signifies predisposing production realities with no dead weight or preconceptions, of being able to elaborate automation as well as ancient crafts, perceived as compatible and integrable phenomena.

Alessandro Mendini, December 1993

RIGHT: Mendini's study of Alessi developments; OPPOSITE: Alessandro Mendini with 'Peyrano' chocolate box, 1990

RICERCA STORICA FILOLOGICA

«PAESAGGIO CASALINGO»

DALISI

TRIENNALE HOLLEIN

BERLINO «CIBI E RITI»

DISEGNI TATEISHI

P6

PORTOGHESI
HOLLEIN
ROSSI
MENDINI
VENTURI
TUSQUETS
GRAVES
MEYER
TIGERMAN
YAMASHITA

PACKAGING SOTTSASS ASSOCIATI

RICERCA DECORO

NAVONE

SAPPER

QUARTETT
THUN
SANTACHIARA
B.D SCARZELLA HAMEL

OGGETTI FORTI

CASTIGLIONI POSATE

SOTTSASS

RIEDIZIONI STORICHE (ANCHE INTERNE)

OFFICINA

MOROZZI

→ ARTIGIANATO
→ ALTRI MATERIALI
→ NUOVA DISTRIBUZIONE

BOLLITORI SAPPER GRAVES

DECORAZIONE

NAVONE
VENTURI

CAFFETTIERA ROSSI

NEO-KITSCH

OGGETTO DEBOLE
IPOTESI DI NUOVA DISTRIBUZIONE

PAESAGGIO CASALINGO

DOMESTIC LANDSCAPE 1977-79

 Soon after meeting Mendini at *Modo*, it occurred to me to present him with another old project of mine, a complete historical-critical research on Alessi and its production. To use the same words that he would use in the introduction to the book of the same name, I was convinced of the fact that 'the critical knowledge of one's own production is the essential condition to be able to project one's own future'.

I also believed that an authoritative text on Alessi's history would be a brilliant communication operation, and that there were the necessary premises at Alessi to formalise our position as part of the phenomenon of 'the Italian design factories'. Mendini accepted, and gladly set himself to work with a few collaborators including Patrizia Rizzi and Patrizia Scarzella. He really did a huge job, which included charts of all our old products. It also marked the occasion for us to start a production museum, gathering, mainly from old employees, examples of old models in exchange for new ones. [The research programme analysed an enormous quantity of company products classifying them according to chronological, typological, technical, functional, aesthetical and economical criteria, and after ten years it still continues to be a definitive reference point for the Alessi metaproject development.]

At the end of the research, which today still constitutes a useful reference for my product policy, Mendini condensed the main parts into a book published by Domus Editoriale with the title *Domestic landscape. The Alessi production from 1921 to 1980*. The book was also the catalogue for the exhibition of the same name that Mendini organised for the XVI Milan Triennale of December 1979.

The installation was designed by the Austrian architect Hans Hollein, it was beautiful and expensive, and we used it again with great success on many future occasions (the last one being the presentation for the *'100 x 100 make up'* operation, in Frankfurt in 1992.

Extract from Alberto Alessi's Factory Journal

OPPOSITE AND BELOW: The exhibition designed by Hans Hollein

TEA AND COFFEE PIAZZA

1983

 An implicit consequence of Mendini's collaboration on the book and the exhibition [*Domestic Landscape*] was his involvement in the future experimentation stages concerning Product and Communication Policy.

Sandro understood how close to my heart this aspect was, and he fostered it with conspiratorial chats and half projects during the two years for which the research lasted. Ever since the final draft for the book, we agreed on including in the chapter dealing with 'Alessi d'après' . . . the announcement of a new, important move: the Programme 6, as the art series programme was then known, would become the 'gymnasium' for our experiments, and we were going to start with a challenging research on the theme of the tea and coffee service, which he rightly considered to be the 'object-symbol' of our sector.

Some of the most interesting 'pure architects' of the world would participate. Each of them would design their own tea and coffee service. Mendini's intention was an explicit reference to the origins of the Italian design phenomenon: even then, in the early fifties, a few 'pure architects' had begun to design objects. There was also another design related motivation: for some time Sandro was preaching and writing that the phenomenon of Italian *bel design* was dying and that something else should take its place.

Ours then, was an attempt conceived to bring an important contribution to the history of design in the eighties, and, it goes without saying, that the idea of writing an important chapter in the history of contemporary design was tremendously attractive to me. I felt as if I was in the eye of the storm!

Mendini had invited 13 architects (Isozaki, who wanted to participate, and came to Crusinallo, couldn't complete his project in time, whilst the Swedish Erskine and the Ticinese Reichlin and Reinhart didn't join us). In practice, every one of them would eventually be labelled a Postmodernist, and I think our venture will pass to history with this title, but I'm not sure if Mendini did it deliberately: rather, I'm inclined to think, that he simply wanted to choose the more interesting figures of the time, and it was by chance that the more interesting ones were those more or less close to the Postmodernist movement . . .

I had explained to the designers that we were leaving two alternative *modi operandi* at their disposal: small-scale artisan production and industrial production. We preferably requested the latter, but didn't exclude the former, to which I was personally tied by an inscrutable ancestral penchant. I must say that practically every one started working with enthusiasm, but theoretically, on the second option. After a few months I began to receive sketches and drawings which filled me with joy: I really felt these were projects that were destined to change the history of design. Mendini was also very happy.

The time came to make a few prototypes, and that is when the problems started. Despite the commitments undertaken and the best intentions of the designers, almost none of the

projects had the necessary characteristics for series production, and the option of small-scale artisan production included by myself in the brief with great bravery and foolhardiness, was in actual fact very difficult to put into practice at Alessi. All our excellent mechanics and model makers, the only people able to work on a small-scale series, were already involved with the construction of the moulds and the prototypes necessary to the ranges already in production.

In addition, Uncle Ettore was very concerned about the projects submitted, from which (in his view, and quite rightly), he expected something a little more concrete, and was beginning to twist his nose with an unmistakable – and well known – movement and meaning . . . Once again, the gap between my idealistic motivations and the reality of what could actually be done at Alessi had evidently emerged!

I felt alone, between the anvil of Mendini and the designers, and the hammer of the factory, and I didn't know what to do . . . Unfairly taking advantage of a long illness of Uncle (the only one in his career, I think, but one which was providential), and with the complicity of chief-engineer Prina, I set part of the workshop to work, and some very interesting prototypes emerged, which nonetheless only increased – together with the interest of Mendini and the designers – my desperation. How could we proceed beyond the prototypes?

My reaction, as usual, was to bide some time, and so it went on, between the visit of a designer and a prototype, for a couple of years.

Eventually, in 1982, under pressure from Mendini who wanted to have an official result from the operation, I decided to hand over the production of the pieces to a number of craftsmen in the Milanese hinterland, who would produce them on our behalf. Through the passionate activity of Patrizia Scarzella and Christina Hamel we were able to put together the first silver prototypes of the projects. The day I received the first group of prototypes I was besides myself with emotion, but also with fear. I realised, in fact, that it was one thing making the prototypes, and another selling these objects, which always resulted in being more exciting from the expressive point of view, but were scarcely functional and extremely expensive. My nervousness was increased by Michele, who was following the proceedings with a lot of concern, and who some time before had warned me about Father's possible reactions ('Now are you going to tell Dad what you're doing?'). Closing my eyes a little, I decided to proceed alone, at least until I had all the first silver prototypes, paying for them out of my pocket. True, I didn't know how all these projects could enter the Alessi universe,

but I was now sure of their quality and the importance of our operation.[1] Backed by Mendini (to whom, though, I never had the courage to confess the state of things within our company), I went ahead. Through an acquaintance of Fulvio Irace, an architectural historian and friend of Sandro's, we got in touch with a New York gallery owner specialising in architectural designs, Max Protetch, who had excellent resources for introduction and promotion in the American market, but no money. Through Bill Schwabel, our distributor at the time in America, we put at his disposal the entire first series of eleven services (the one I paid for out of my own pocket), with which Protetch organised a large operation of presentations in museums throughout the USA. I won't say anything more about this initiative. The services were numbered from one to 99, plus three artist's proofs, and sold at astronomical prices . . . It wasn't a commercially viable operation from the sales point of view. But it was a ground breaking operation in our history.

The Tea and Coffee Piazza was introduced in Milan during the ICSID Congress in September 1983 . . . it really was a great triumph, a move that shook the more advanced design companies at the time, that took by surprise the most aware magazines, and that still now is remembered in our environment as a text book operation for the efficiency of its research and communication.

The Tea and Coffee Piazza gave us a definitive international presence, both in the view of the media and of the most influential outlets in the world. As a matter of fact, besides starting the trend for strongly expressive, Postmodern and 'style-symbol' designer objects, which became the typical trait of the most interesting design of the eighties, it allowed me to build up a formidable amount of contacts and experiences which would prove valuable for the product policies and the communication of the following years.
Extract from Alberto Alessi's Factory Journal

With great innovation and creativity the Alessi company has introduced a line of products which have a great appeal not only to design conscious consumers but to the general public whose awareness of quality motivates their purchases. Alessi has been responsible for elevating the general level of design around the world by serving as an inspiration for other design companies to create items of distinction in order to keep up with the quality of Alessi. I am honoured to be among the many designers who have created work for Alessi production.   Richard Meier, November 1993

1   Sottsass, when he came to Crusinallo some time before, had shown great enthusiasm for Aldo Rossi's prototypes: 'One has to be a great designer to have this courage!' he declared, which was a great comfort to me.

RIGHT FROM ABOVE: Drawings and prototypes by: Alessandro Mendini; Robert Venturi; Aldo Rossi; Paolo Portoghesi; Stanley Tigerman; OPPOSITE: Prototypes; PAGE 40 FROM ABOVE: Michael Graves; Charles Jencks; Hans Hollein; PAGE 41 FROM ABOVE: Richard Meier; Alessandro Mendini; Paolo Portoghesi; PAGE 42 FROM ABOVE: Aldo Rossi; Stanley Tigerman; PAGE 43 FROM ABOVE: Oscar Tusquets; Robert Venturi; Kazumasa Yamashita

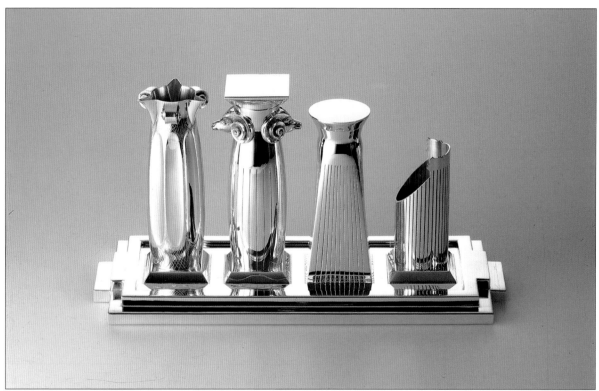

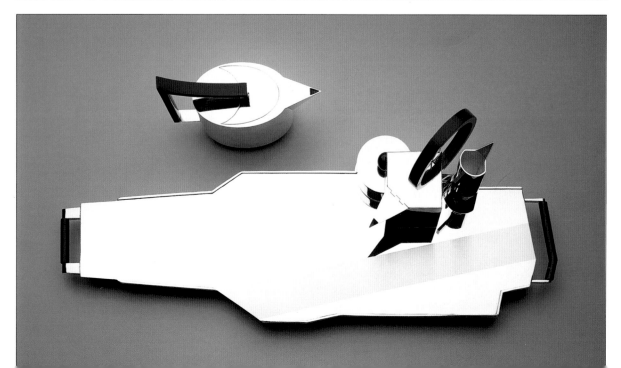

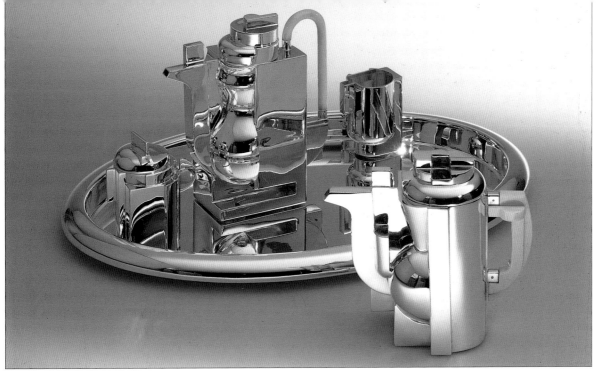

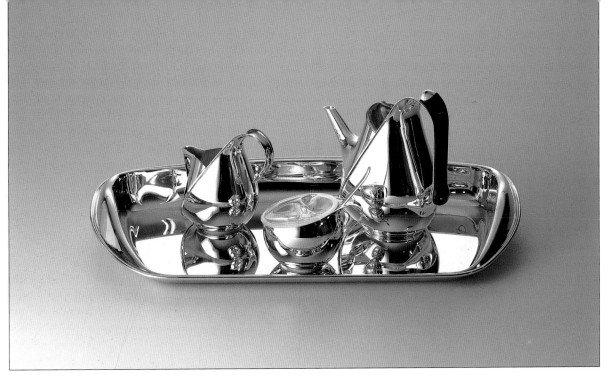

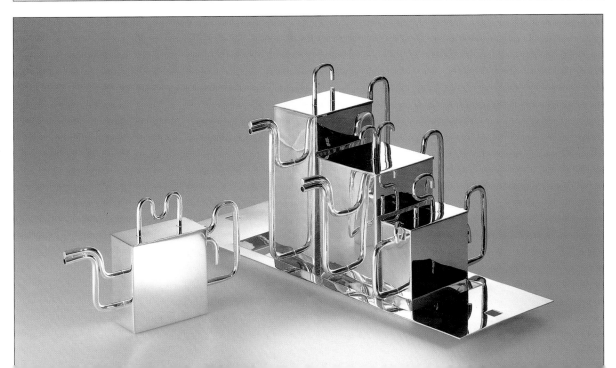

OFFICINA ALESSI
1983-

 The creation of the Officina Alessi trade mark of Alessi spa in 1983 to co-exist alongside the trade mark Alessi, was to identify an aspect of the company's activity that in the past had often remained on paper or at first prototype stage: namely the wish to research and experiment with innovations of form, style, function and methods of manufacture, free from the limits usually imposed by industrial mass production. Alessi's intention was to offer a keen and culturally curious public a wide spectrum of proposals employing both sophisticated industrial technology and typical handicraft processes, and utilising traditional metals – such as nickel silver, brass and copper – but also silver and tin chosen not for their intrinsic value but to match the characteristics of each design. With the co-operation of retailers it is the company's objective to offer the public the results of research carried out by some of the most interesting figures on the contemporary international industrial design scene. According to the circumstances, these results will take the form of standard production, or limited series, or even of unique pieces; not developed as a rival but as a complement to the Alessi production (which proceeds on its own course of developing mass-produced articles for the general public). The new production comes from the same factory in Crusinallo and its skilled and experienced staff, and is aimed at a more sophisticated and complex contemporary market. It is divided today into eight series, significantly different from each other in terms of content, production, materials and price: Antologia Alessi; Alessi d'après; Tea and Coffee Piazza; La Tavola di Babele; Archivi; 'La Cintura di Orione' and La Casa della Felicità; and Tendentse.

LEFT: Selection of Officina products

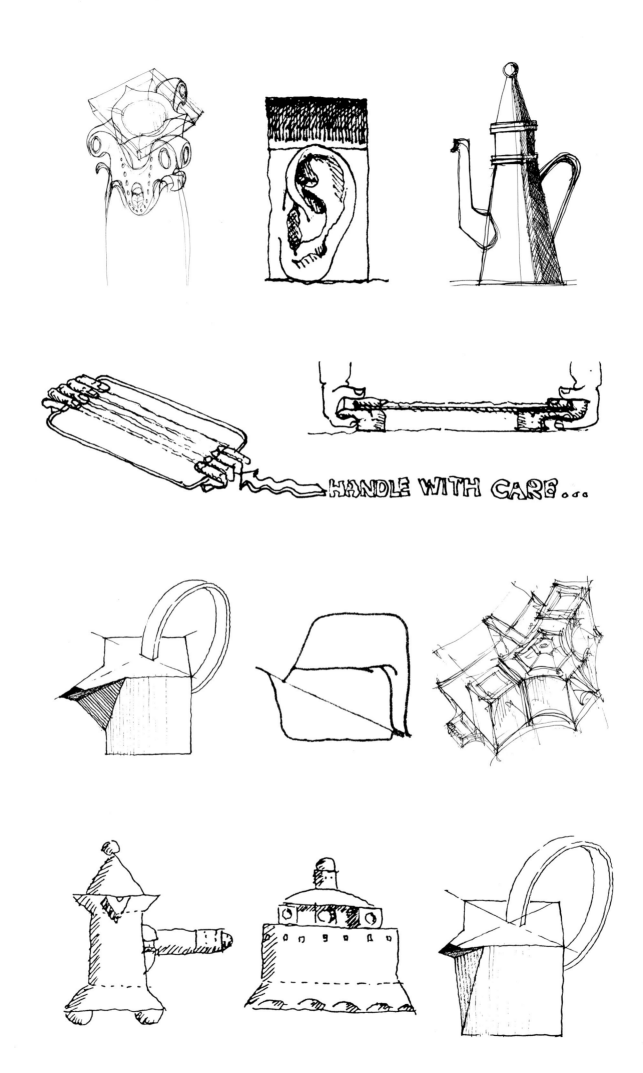

HANDLE WITH CARE...

problem is no longer that of occupying an environment, but only of managing it in the best possible way. For this purpose the performances of individuals can be bettered, to allow the fullest and most far-reaching exploitation of their environment. Strategy K thus involves, for every generation, the production of a small number of costly, that is complex individuals capable of storing information and of generating behaviour very carefully adapted to their social and natural environment. Strategy r is adopted for new ecological niches and highly unstable environments, where recurrent catastrophes destroy populations. The real question, then, is no longer how to invest in the individual as such, but the rapidity with which the environment can be repopulated.

Concerning evolution times, strategy r necessitates an early ripening, because everything that delays reproduction entails a loss of resources and time. Conversely, strategy K is favoured by long periods of maturation during which information necessary to the production of complex individuals can be processed. Early maturation leads to a specialisation and decrease in flexibility, allowing the experimentation of 'new forms of exceptional freedom'. The delayed somatologic development, typical of strategy K, produces candidates for an evolutive transformation. In this way the capacity for adaptation is retained, enabling diversity to be developed.

In our contemporary situation domestic goods live prevalently within strategy r, geared to indiscriminate reproduction. To combat this state of affairs, action must be taken to impose a selective, K-type strategy. This can be done by studying the appearance of 'precious individuals' within a population, so that complex multi-operations can work together. For this reason the theoretical task of research is to develop a design methodology with the capacity to reformulate the sphere of action on single elements.

In this basic definition, a map of relations between objects and operations becomes an analytical tool for establishing a field of theoretical experimentation, where more complex functional areas can be picked out.

Therefore the principal task is to indicate a methodological path, from which the criteria needed for the search for new types of objects can be obtained.

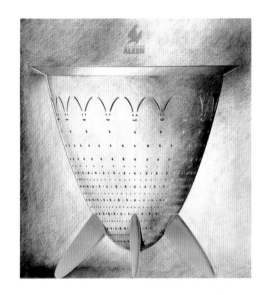

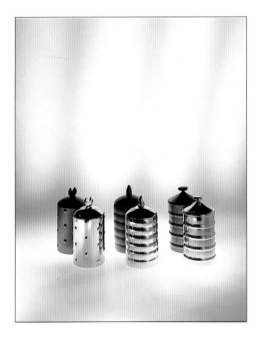

RIGHT FROM ABOVE: Design sketch for 'Max le Chinois', Philippe Starck; 'Lady Momento' watch, Aldo Rossi, 1988; 'Kalisto' kitchen containers, Clare Brass, 1992-93 (Memory Containers); OPPOSITE FROM ABOVE: Original design sketches for the Tea and Coffee Piazza by: Charles Jencks, Stanley Tigerman, Aldo Rossi, Stanley Tigerman, Hans Hollein, Oscar Tusquets, Paolo Portoghesi, Michael Graves, Michael Graves, Hans Hollein; PAGE 46 FROM ABOVE L TO R: 'Girevole', Pietro Consagra, 1975; 'Multimodel-X', Dusan Dzamonja, 1974; 'Guscio n1', Gio Pomodoro, 1972; 'Narciso', Andrea Cascella, 1977; 'Forma orizzontale circolare', Carmelo Cappello, 1974 (all Alessi d'après)

NEAPOLITAN COFFEEMAKER
RICCARDO DALISI (1987)

 During a frugal working lunch at a restaurant below his place, sometime in 1979, Mendini mentioned a friend of his, a strange Neapolitan architect who, having heard of our operation on tea and coffee services . . . wanted to present us with a project for a Neapolitan cafetiere.

As usual Mendini dropped it casually, and naturally I was enthusiastic about the idea. There's nothing to be surprised about, I've never declined an invitation of Sandro's, and I've never regretted doing so: it must also be said that when he made a suggestion I would think carefully about it . . . naturally, after that it's up to me to work out if and how to proceed with the venture.

I would never have thought of meeting someone like Dalisi, shy and sweet, as if he had come out of an Italian neorealist film of the fifties, arriving in Milan and feeling so estranged he could have been in New York. Someone who, during the nine years the project lasted, literally submerged me with prototypes of tin coffee makers, which today represent one of the 'tastier' parts of our ideal Museum.

In this case too, the story went the usual way: a great weariness on behalf of our establishment, problems in getting in tune with the designer, difficulties in finalising the definitive project . . . all the same, even if the Neapolitan never achieved a great public success, I certainly don't regret this collaboration which amongst other things has enjoyed a long and relevant period of international notoriety.

Dalisi is a figure of high poetic intensity, who has introduced a sense of sweetness and docility as a new anthropological dimension to the Alessi industry at the right moment, and who is now working with us on wood and porcelain.
Extract from Alberto Alessi's Factory Journal

The Project
The research into the Neapolitan coffee maker, which began in 1979 and officially ended in 1987, was the longest in the history of the Alessi company. Beginning with a vast socio-anthropological survey on the way in which the coffee maker was used and how coffee was perceived in the small towns of the Neapolitan hinterland, the project produced over the years – aside from the many pages of writing and sketches – dozens and dozens of prototypes (in the end 200), all different from one another, all perfectly operative, all made of tin. Dalisi made them, working with that curious craftsman, Don Vincenzo . . .

Our first reactions were . . . of surprise and at times of scorn – the use of tin, a poor, low-grade material by definition, the ingenuous approach to designing coffee makers, with the useless philological attention to construction detail typical of the man/utensil rather than the machine/man, hence probably unusable in mass production, the same popular formal inspiration, caricatural, anthropomorphic and therefore far from 'Bel Design', made these prototypes apparently unsuitable to be seriously produced in a factory . . .

Then over the years, a sort of miracle took place – as the innumerable prototypes began to stack up on the shelves and on the tables of the Technical Office . . . something began to scratch away at our *Weltanschauung* . . . under the prolonged though innocuous siege of little men, saints, animals and bizarre coffee makers, Dalisi managed to cut into our industrial security. Bit by bit, with a forced but – I believe – effective osmosis between the two worlds of crafts and industry, our Neapolitan coffee maker was born.
Alberto Alessi

RIGHT FROM ABOVE: Dalisi with prototype (not Alessi), variations on the theme; OPPOSITE BACKGROUND IMAGE: Prototype coffee maker; INSET:

Neapolitan coffee maker, 1987; PAGES 58-59 BACKGROUND IMAGE: Prototype coffee makers; INSET: Initial sketches

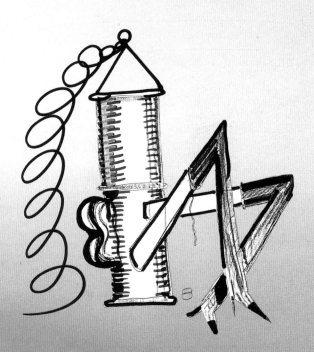

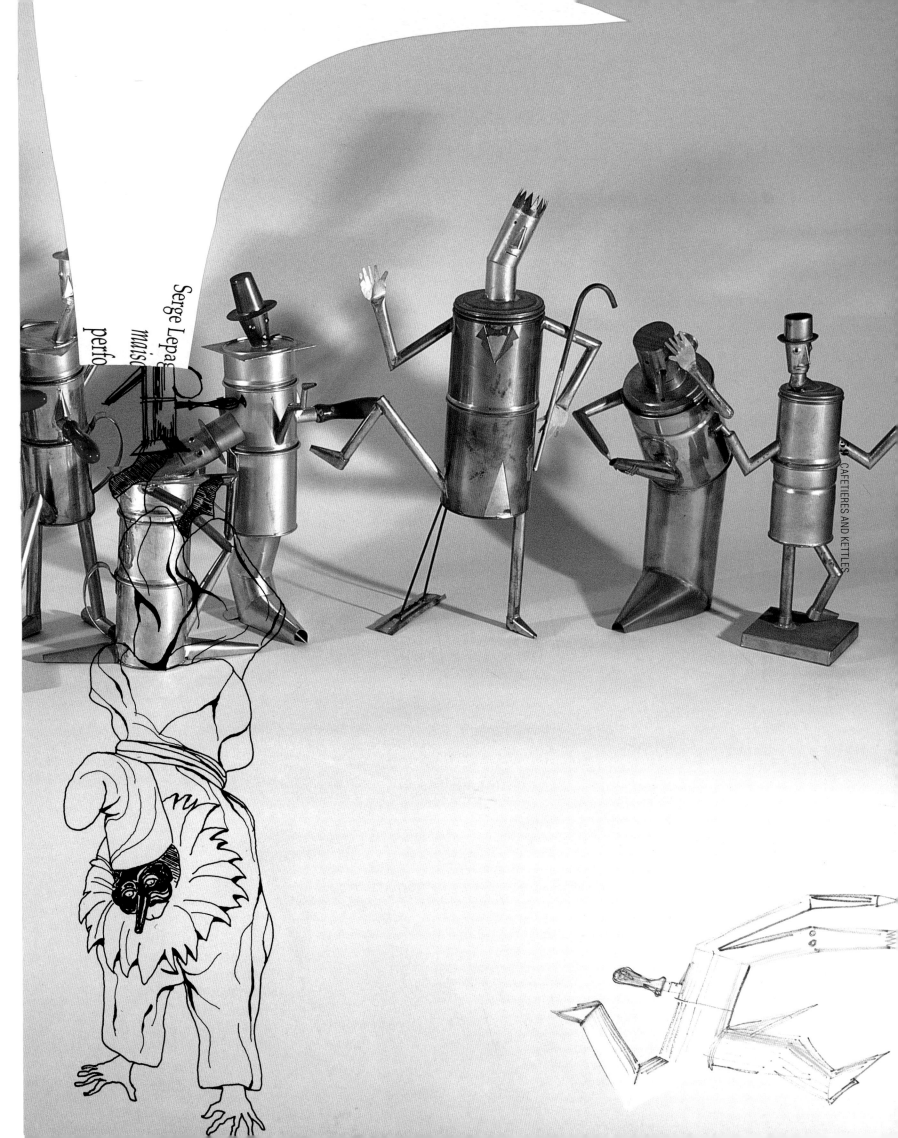

Serge Lepa
maiso
perfo

FAMILIAL CONNECTIONS

MICHAEL GRAVES CONSIDERS HIS RELATIONSHIP WITH ALESSI

 We are fortunate to have a long and prosperous association with Alessi. Our relationship began over 20 years ago with an invitation to design a formal, sterling silver tea service, and has since grown from the teakettle which followed the tea service into an entire family of objects for the kitchen and the table. Each time we complete another Alessi project, I cannot help but wonder what distinguishes Alessi from the many other companies that produce similar items, and how this contributes to our ongoing mutual success.

Throughout my career I have been interested in continuities, whether they are continuities of culture, aesthetics or technique. I always look forward to the challenges of setting up new ones, as well as extending those that already exist. For this reason, when asked to reflect and comment upon the work that my firm has done with Alessi, I consider it in a similar way. The association between Michael Graves Architects and Alessi, and the manner in which we approach the design of our products, have much in common. This can be seen in our overall history as designer and manufacturer, and more specifically within that history's particular events.

A number of years ago I was invited, along with several other architects from around the world, to participate in an Alessi project named the Tea and Coffee Piazza. The exercise, as described by Alessi, called for us to consider the relationships between the following things: an archetype of domestic housewares (the coffee and tea service); the realm of architecture; and our own ideas regarding design. Beyond the exercise itself, the wonderful thing about the project was that we would be able to see our designs realised; handcrafted in sterling silver and made available in limited production. The Tea and Coffee Piazza provided Alessi with an occasion to introduce itself to the North American market as a manufacturer of both high design and high quality items. For the architects it was an opportunity to take part in a provocative project, one that was outside the range of work normally encountered. In addition, the overall timing of the project could not have been better. The economy was thriving, especially in the United States, and architecture and design were enjoying renewed popular attention, as well as diversity in their own internal debates.

The tea service, unlike other projects we were later to be involved in, had few if any design restrictions. It was like a small test. You had to fulfil your design intentions while maintaining the typology of the tea service. The set was to consist of five pieces: serving tray, creamer and sugar bowl, a teapot which was to be less squat, and a taller more vertical coffee pot. We never discussed the cost of materials or issues of fabrication. Essentially, we enjoyed *carte blanche*. Alessi, it seemed, was willing to give us the necessary freedoms so that the appearance of each Tea and Coffee Piazza would in no way be compromised.

Before being approached to do the Tea and Coffee Piazza, I had had little knowledge of Alessi, its history, or the extent of its production. I had seen the Richard Sapper teakettle, although I had never associated it with Alessi's name. Upon hearing this from me, Alessi must have concluded that it was unlikely that the company's name would be recognised by many other people, especially those who were not related to the design profession. In order to cease this identification problem, Alessi arranged to have the collection of Tea and Coffee Piazzas exhibited in museums and galleries across the United States, places such as the Metropolitan Museum of Art and the Max Protetch Gallery (both in New York) so that the Alessi name and field of work could be introduced to the desired audience and market. In addition to this, placing the tea services within the context of a museum provided instant status: they were recognised as objects which were part of a long history of decorative arts and, correspondingly, they were seen as objects of value. These were qualities which in turn would become associated with other Alessi products as well.

It was following the success of the tea service exhibition that I was asked to join Alessi in another venture. The idea was to produce a teakettle specifically for the North American market. For this, it was determined that an American designer was necessary. Americans, Alessi told me, need a kettle to boil water for their instant coffee, whereas Italians, French and Spanish drink espresso almost exclusively, and therefore don't have any need for a teakettle, aside from an occasional cup of tea. (In the end, however, the teakettle did very well both in the United States and in Europe). With this in mind we began our second Alessi project.

The requirements and expectations for this new American kettle were much different from those of the tea service, as was the manner in which we went about it. It began with books that Alessi had compiled, books that provided a visual history of the teakettle, with the purpose of avoiding design problems that Alessi had encountered in its

previous kettles. We were asked to design a kettle whose body was formed in such a way that it could accept and maintain a large volume of water at its base, nearest the flame. The handle was not to extend over the pot's side, so it would not be exposed to the direct heat of the cooking surface. It was only after we had a solution to these functional requirements that we could begin to think about the character of the kettle, the associations it would conjure up – in other words, how the aesthetic and functional aspects of design could be brought together into a whole. Whereas the objective for the Tea and Coffee Piazza had been to showcase design and invention in an aesthetic sense, the priority of the teakettle was to resolve pragmatic design issues, and then to produce an attractive and interesting object.

Such a distinction between projects is representative of Alessi's clarity of intention and purpose in the conception of its work. It also indicates the importance that is given to the notion of typology, and the relationship of current work to the greater historical context of decorative arts. Whenever Alessi visits my office to discuss a project, a conversation will undoubtedly arise on the subject of typology, provoked by a connection detail or perhaps the ball which is the base of the fruit bowl we are now working on. The concentrated attention given to this small element and the knowledge that our visitor shares with us about it, reveals his and Alessi's true captivation and affection for the subject. This is not surprising when you discover that Alessi holds a tradition of documenting and publishing its work; in catalogues, press books and picture books; books that always begin with a history of the company, its founding and its work. The significance of the Tea and Coffee Piazza is not surprising in this context.

Alessi considers each new project as one that will continue and enrich its tradition of design and production. The wisdom of the company is in recognising that a teakettle can be more than an efficient device for boiling water; it can have an iconic value as well. Alessi also understands that every object has a history; as a form, as an instrument and as a crafted piece. But perhaps most importantly, with Alessi, tradition extends to the idea of family. As a designer you and your people are brought in and treated as members of a family – it's a very personal relationship of designer and manufacturer. Ultimately this is what ties everything and everyone together so beautifully, and what provides such distinction for Alessi.

RIGHT FROM ABOVE L TO R: Condiment sets, 1994; cafetiere, butter dish, coffee cups and spoons, 1989-93; round plate, 1991, tray with handles, 1990, and pitcher, 1991; OPPOSITE: Kettle with a bird shaped whistle, 1985, sugar bowl, 1988-92, creamer, 1988-92, salt and pepper set, 1988-93; PAGE 62: The Graves family

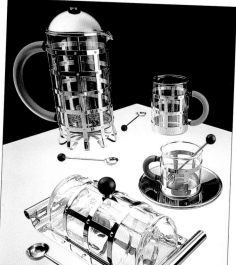

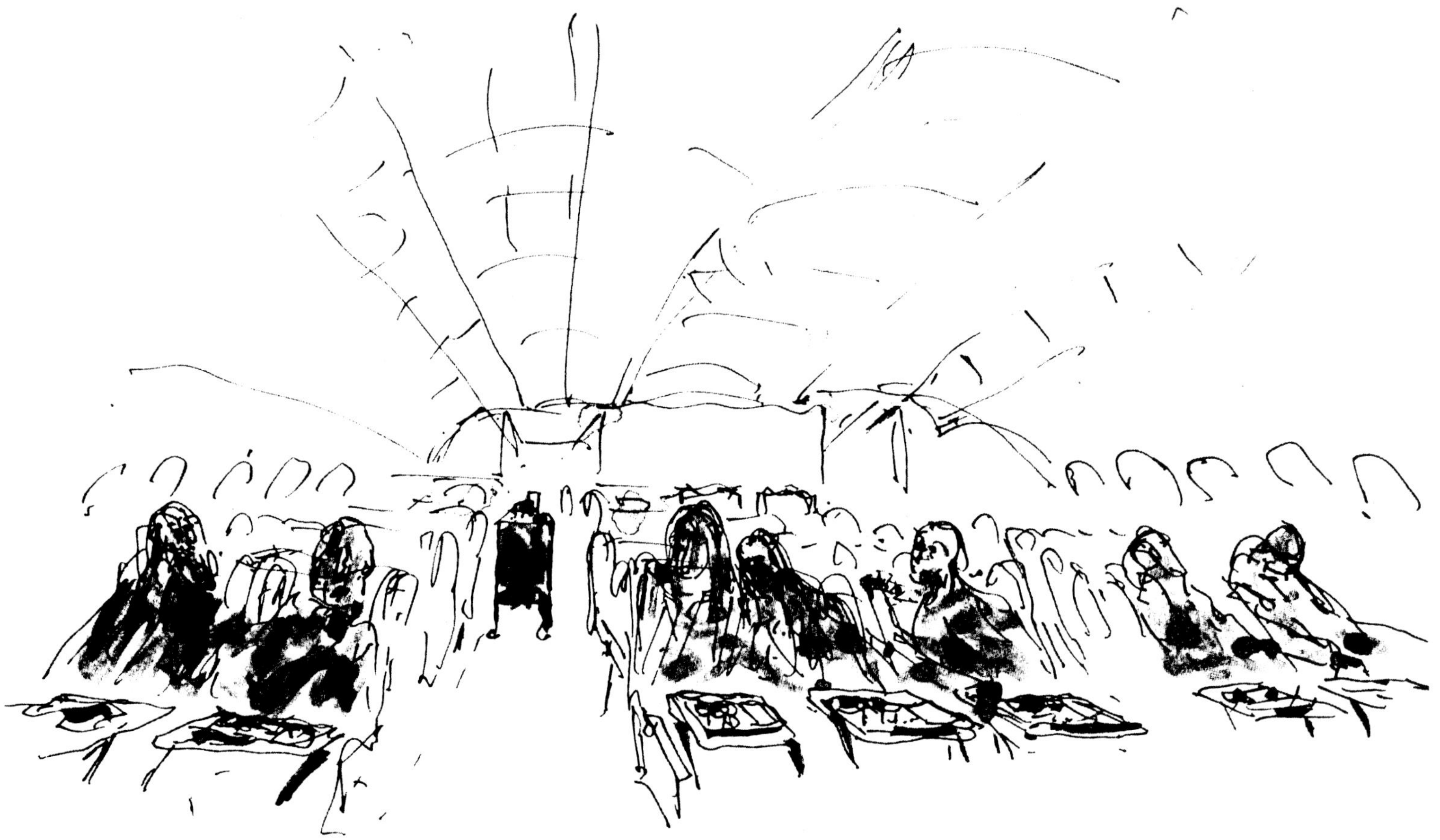

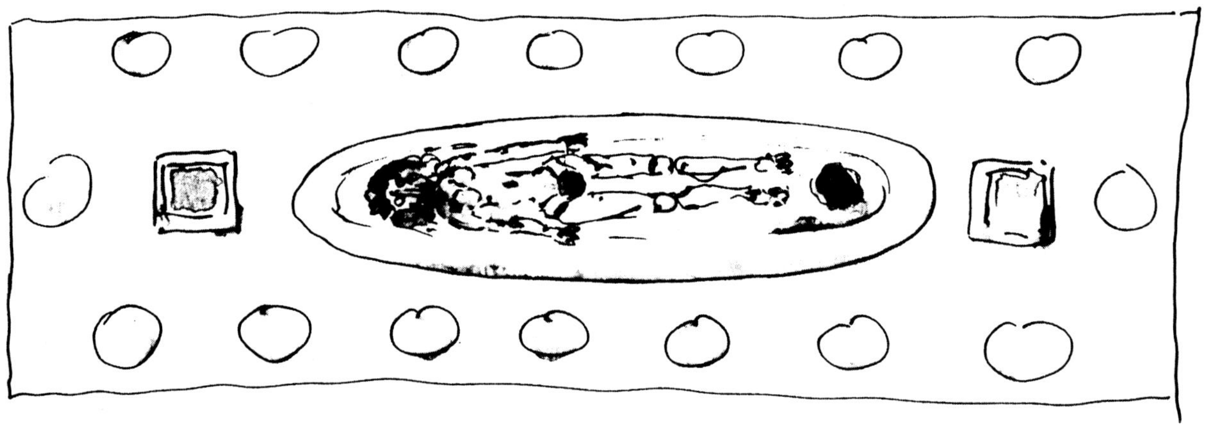

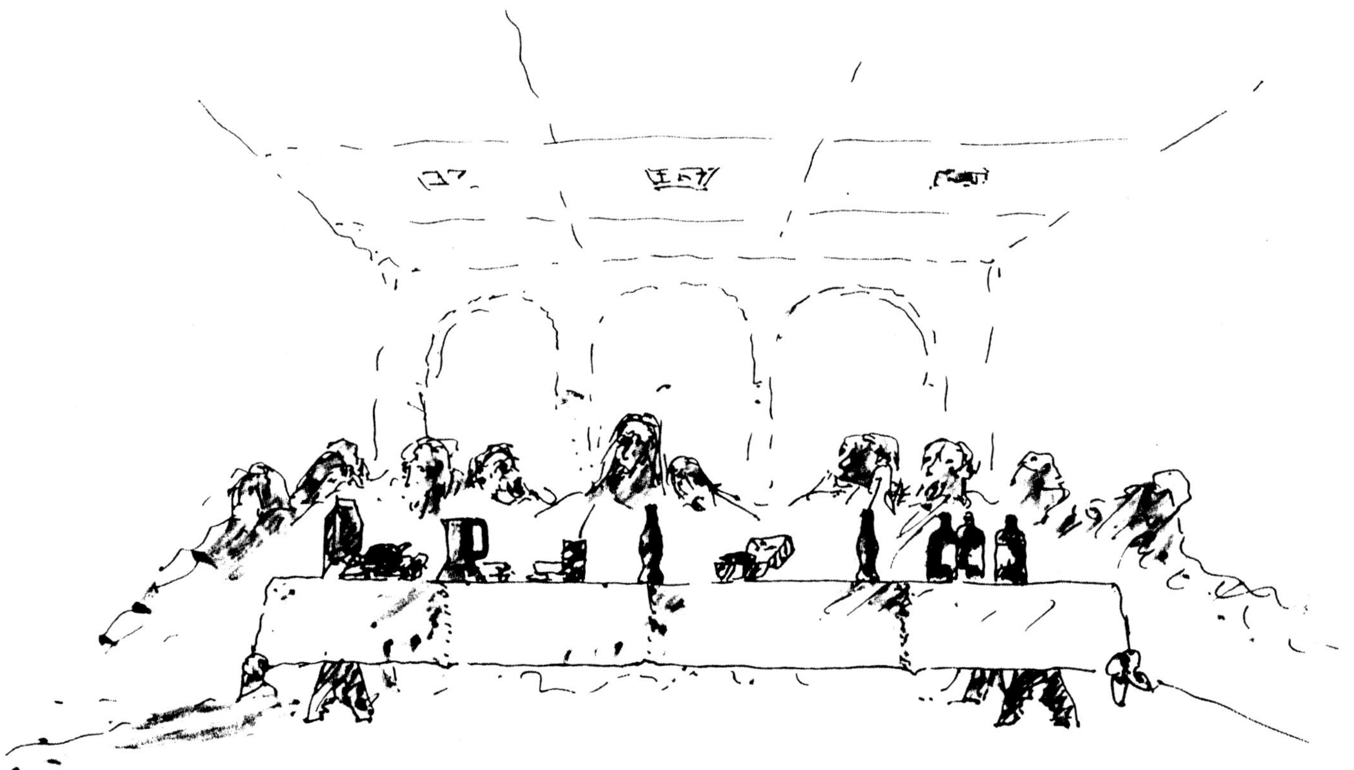

CIBI E RITI

FOOD AND RITUAL 1981

The design seminar *Cibi e Riti* was born from an idea of Alessandro Mendini and Francois Burkhardt on the occasion of the third edition of the *Paesaggio Casalingo* exhibition, held in Berlin in January 1981, with an installation by Achille Castiglioni. The idea was to begin research on new themes and rituals of living, with the intention of defining possible new typologies and objects for the home. Apart from Sapper, Sottsass and Hollein, other designers were invited, chosen from a heterogeneous expressive context: the Viennese Peter Kubelka, man of cinema but also a gastronomist, the French stylist Jean Charles de Castelbajac, Peter Cook, British architect, founding member of 'Archigram', and Stefan Wewerka, experimental designer and great mime artist.

The proceedings were organised and co-ordinated by Alessandro Mendini, Francois Burkhardt and Alberto Alessi with the collaboration of Patrizia Scarzella.

From the perspective of tangible results, the seminar was a confirmation of the likely impossibility of creating a new typology of domestic objects for mankind in the twentieth century. This was especially true in a sector like Alessi's, so strongly influenced by the collective memory, and where, in fact, the typologies in use are centuries old, sometimes millennia, and the most recent 'real' innovation is the espresso cafetiere born in Italy in the thirties. The results of the seminar were published in a book of the same name. In his introduction to *Cibi e Riti*, Alessandro Mendini writes:

'Eating' is an 'action', which is performed consciously or unconsciously by the person. The survival of the species is realised through instinctive and primal action: first, breathing; second, eating; third, sleeping; fourth, expelling excreta. If a person doesn't perform these actions, he is either dying or is dead. Air, food and rest are indispensable to life. Then, a person performs other important actions: he sees, listens, talks, tastes, smells and makes love. With these ten primordial actions, people assume their role of 'inhabitants' in the world, in other words of beings that surround themselves with tools and spaces suitable to improve the quality of their actions. Therefore, 'inhabiting' is mankind's eleventh primal action: the world is a great house, the largest house, made up of increasingly smaller rooms. To execute the primal actions with confidence, conscience and pleasure, mankind performs an infinite number of other actions: cooking, seducing, singing, travelling, killing, washing, drinking tea, buying medicines, reading papers, going on vacation, building industries etc. But the search for air, food and rest remain the fundamental needs of humanity, after the distant end of that mythological habitat deprived of objects: the Garden of Eden . . . *Laura Polinoro*

In his beginnings, Alberto Alessi – inspired by a few architects and designers – developed a vision which went beyond pure mercantile pragmatism. In this period, the concern was not only the development – or reinterpretation – of household-goods, but rather the search for a cultural approach to matters and objects of daily life.

In such a way the first discussions, meetings and projects, (very often initiated by Sandro Mendini), were prototypical investigations into a subject, an object, a topic, a situation – a vision and idea of the future.

At this time I not only developed products but also conceived and designed the first exhibitions on the 'new' Alessi – at the Triennale as well as at the Brera in Milan. The Programme 6, the Tea and Coffee Piazza evolved, I contributed the 'Aircraft-carrier'. Also I was instrumental in such interdisciplinary brain storming sessions as the famous design week Cibi e Riti *at Francois Burkhardt's Design Center in Berlin (with Sottsass, Castelbajac, Kubelka and Sapper) a type of event which unfortunately was never repeated. At the same time I worked on the design of a filter (Melitta) coffee-maker, and cooking moulds as a modern reinterpretation of traditional items, forms of high geometrical complexity. Investigation into new materials, different production methods and multiple applications brought these objects to a high degree of perfection but then never realisation. Alessi's direction, in part highly successful, is now entering a cultural borderline. A new Alessi-vision is asked for.* Hans Hollein, April 1994

ABOVE AND OPPOSITE: Hollein's designs made during the seminar at the IDZ in Berlin, January 1981

THE PASTA-SET

MASSIMO MOROZZI (1985)

In the summer of 1982, after a year and a half of meetings and chats, Morozzi showed me the design for the Pasta-set. Morozzi maintained that it would have been interesting to concentrate on Mediterranean cooking objects for 'making pasta' and, at the same time, 'to let pasta be discovered'.

It has to be said that the solution of a boiling pan with an internal colander isn't a new one, because there are traces of it in a sixteenth-century text by Scappi, but as far as private use and gift objects go it was a totally new idea.

I was interested in the idea of working with Morozzi because of his experience in radical design (ie: the 'Archizoom' experience), but also for his decision to become a designer in the 'classical' sense, accepting the reasoning of marketing as a component in his work.

In his practices there was hardly any interest in the formal aspect; the form can be read, in the final designing stages, as a deduction.

It was the actual form of the object that caused initial perplexities, despite the revolutionary idea: its functionalism was tested, but it couldn't be recognised as a boiling pan. So we decided to test the public's approach to the object: through a market research institute, we organised a series of interviews which we observed directly from a two-way mirror. About fifty per cent of the people questioned didn't recognise the Pasta-set as a boiling pan, giving it very diverse connotations, whilst the remaining fifty per cent liked the idea.

The results weren't entirely positive but we decided to go into production, and rightly so, because it became immensely popular, and in the following years it influenced the market enormously today I believe there are about a hundred copies of the 'Pasta-set' worldwide.   *Alberto Alessi*

In 1990, after the Pasta-set experience, the Vapor-set was launched, designed by Morozzi with the collaboration of Gualtiero Marchesi.

'LA CINTURA DI ORIONE'

RICHARD SAPPER (1979-86)

 In 1979, for the first time in the history of the company, Alessi set themselves the goal of producing a complete cookware set, 'La Cintura di Orione', which was to be the initial corpus of the most advanced line of cooking utensils ever mass produced.

We had, in fact, identified an interesting sector of the market which . . . had been overlooked by the majority of international manufacturers of metal cookware: that of the so-called 'private gourmets', in other words, lovers of intelligent, creative cuisine.

Furthermore, recent Western manufacturing tradition developed ignoring a large number of 'fixed points' which practice in previous periods appeared to have consolidated; the market for mass production was – and still is – dominated by stainless steel with heat-diffusing bases. This metal spread rapidly after the Second World War despite being a bad heat conductor, thanks to the unquestionable advantages of hygiene, easy cleaning and mechanical resistance.

From the fifties, on the assumption that stainless steel should be universally employed, manufacturers produced whole series of kitchen utensils with typological features widely accepted by the public, even though they were the result of a rather generic analysis of consumer requirements. In their

wake . . . the swarm of present-day manufacturers have done nothing but repeat them with a few changes.

Even today, if all goes well, the imagination of international manufacturers – even allowing for the use of other materials: Lagostina, Barazzoni, Sambonet, Opa Oy and Zani for stainless steel; Copco, Lauffer and Le Creuset for cast iron; Arabia and Dansk Design for ceramics; Jensen for silver-plated copper – has not gone any further than a good designer giving the line a structural unity, thus necessarily limiting his action to the facade. In such cases, the greatest limitation is the adoption of the same 'line' or 'form' for all the items in a series, and the use of the same material (each manufacturer's typical one) without taking into account the frequent contra-indications deriving from the different methods of cooking the utensils are intended for.

This analysis of the present situation was the starting point of our research (co-ordinated by Alberto Gozzi (gastronomic expert in charge of professional specialisation courses at the school for Hoteliers, Stresa), Franco Alessi and Richard Sapper, which set out with a wide historical survey on the subject, proceeding to scheduling interviews with professionals in the field, the study of books and printed matter, and the collection of a large number of old utensils.

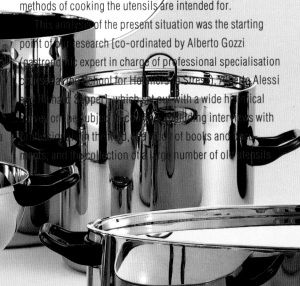

which are to form the nucleus of a future museum. Above all, from the very outset, our study involved not only a great designer [Richard Sapper], but some of the most renowned representatives of the 'great European cuisine': from France Alain Chapel, Raymond Thuilier, Pierre and Michel Troisgros, and Roger Vergé . . . [and] from Italy, Gualtiero Marchesi and Angelo Paracucchi. (Besides being called upon for general consultation to define the appropriate entire series, they were also asked to select certain utensils, on which to work together with Richard Sapper on an individual project).

In their role of chef-designers, these people lost no time in alerting us to the importance of acquiring a sound knowledge of 'cooking techniques' . . . in order to achieve a correct cooking, both gastronomically and nutritionally speaking . . . That is why, on the specific indication of our chef-designers, our series of cooking utensils is a mixed and eclectic one. It consists of utensils made not only of one but several metals (each in the most appropriate metal for the method of cooking to be used) and with shapes not governed solely by aesthetic considerations but strictly related to the cooking requirements of . . . each utensil (thus, utensils differ widely one from another: being conical,

trunc... and cylindrical with rounded edges).

...sing, therefore, that a determining factor in ...nge of utensils has been the choice of metal. ...eel, a poor heat conductor, has been used for the ... (used mainly for boiling water or liquids in general ...t any special heat conducting requirements), for the ...ander and 'Chinois', but also for all lids, handles and knobs. On the other hand, a special laminate of very thick copper (ensuring perfect heat conduction along the entire surface of the pan) with a thin layer of stainless steel on the inside (ensuring maximum hygiene, ease of cleaning but which, because of its limited thickness, does not interfere with the heat conduction ensured by the copper) has been used for all items for delicate cooking processes where temperatures must be controlled and uniform throughout the utensil — for the casserole, cassolette and 'Sauteuse' for risottos, sautéing and sauces. Black steel, with its irreplaceable thermoregulating properties, is the metal used for the frying pan, and egg and crêpe pan . . . Finally, very heavy black enamelled cast iron has been used for the oval casserole, the prince of utensils for slow cooking (pot roasting and stews) requiring steady, moderate heat transmission — a prerogative of this material. *Alberto Alessi*

'FALSTAF'
ALESSANDRO MENDINI (1985-89)

From the moment the last choices were made in defining the appearance of 'La Cintura di Orione', before its launch in 1986, it was clear that it was a series that took its place in a niche market: because of its high cost and the high quality materials used to produce cooking utensils of the highest quality.

'La Cintura di Orione', moreover, represented an important statement for Alessi, as for the first time since the Pasta-set it allowed the company to prosper as a manufacturer of a truly complete series of cooking utensils. During that period, Alessi and Mendini decided to set up an alternative research programme with a view to creating a new series of pans that could be introduced into a lower level of the market and which would re-enter the traditional, technological sector of pans made from stainless steel with an aluminium bottom: a series of pans accessible to an ever growing public, in contrast to the 'La Cintura di Orione' series. It would have to represent a new wave for the consolidation of technical production evolved over decades and by now proving to be saddened by the anonymous large series. To be able to realise a series of pans at contained costs, it was necessary to produce them in an automated production line system. For this reason the production of the bodies of the pans was subcontracted to a specialist production company.

It was clear that technological constraints would limit expressive possibilities, and for this reason it was necessary to seek the collaboration of an adaptable designer, prepared to accept them and even to become an integral part in their strategic planning.

The lid of the series is designed like a cone with a cherry shaped knob. Mendini initiated an international competition for the development of a small article to go on top of the cone, a sort of tiny temple-like monument. Four international architects: Yuri Soloviev (Russian), Michael Graves (American), Arata Isozaki (Japanese) and Philippe Starck (European) were invited to participate in the competition. They all designed an optional feature for the knob handle.

'Falstaf' designed by Mendini and Giorgio Gregori was launched on 7 September 1989 in the Officina Alessi showroom in Milan.

It is unique in being the only series of pans around which a kitchen was designed: as during the course of research, an opportunity with Mendini and Christina Hamel arose to make the first designs for a built-in gas hob and two electric ovens. *Laura Polinoro*

BACKGROUND IMAGE: 'Falstaf' collection; INSET FROM ABOVE L TO R: Knobs by Philippe Starck, Arata Isozaki, Yuri Soloviev, Michael Graves

'LA CUBICA' COOKING BOX
ALDO ROSSI, (1991)

Designed from 1988, Aldo Rossi's 'La Cubica' is produced in PTFE-treated aluminium casting and colour anthracite. It measures 17 by 22 centimetres, and is 19 centimetres high.

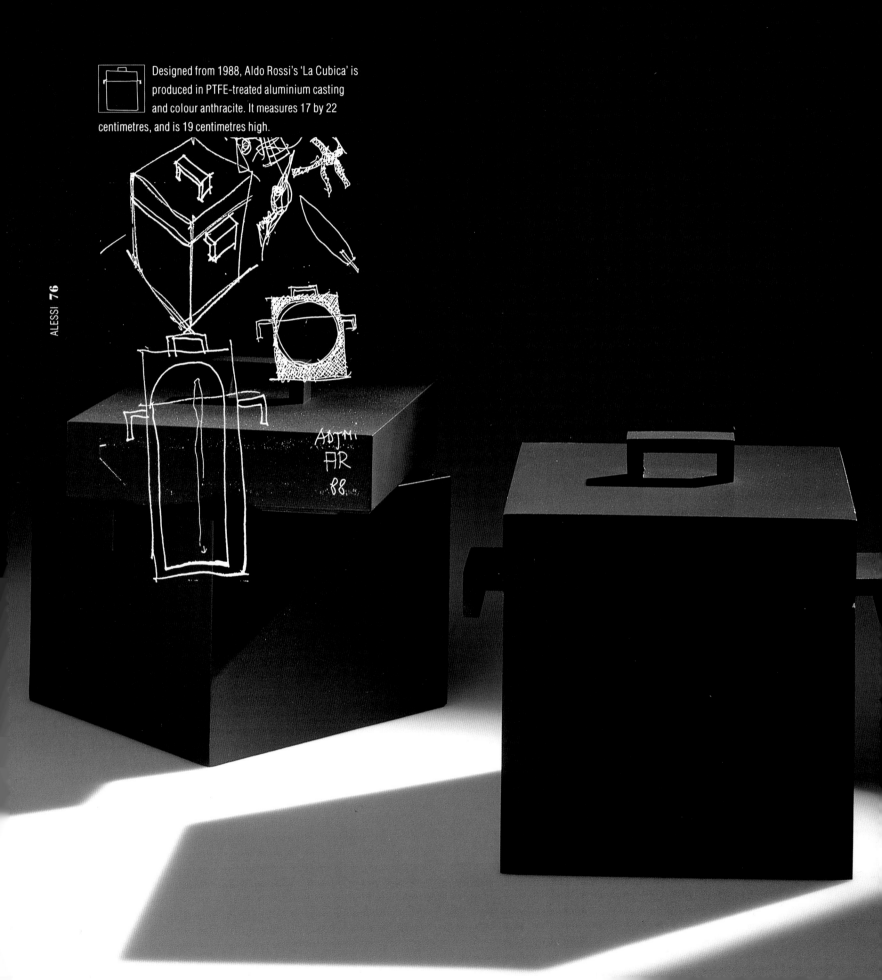

'CACCIA' FLATWARE

*LUIGI CACCIA DOMINIONI, LIVIO
AND PIER GIACOMO CASTIGLIONI (1938) 1990-92*

 The historic exhibitions mounted at the Milan Triennale between 1930 and 1940 provided the background and showcase for the beginnings of Italian design. In the Triennale of 1940, within the 'Mostra dei metalli e dei vetri' directed by architect Ignazio Gardella, the initial signs of a renewal were visible in the area of 'domestic landscape'. On view was a series of cutlery and tableware of a new conception which included Caccia Dominioni and the Castiglioni brothers' highly successful 'Caccia' flatware, in sets of silver and aluminium, and two in ceramic and vermeil. They were the result not only of an expressive but of an extensive renewal of this production sector, now being steadily industrialised through the adoption of new technologies (moulding and die-casting) and the use of new materials such as steel. Giò Ponti wrote in *Domus* (no 150, 1940):

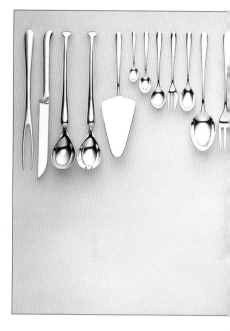

> This Triennale has presented new 'types' of cutlery of such great style, of such purity of form and design as to make me declare that nowhere, in the output of any other country, does any more beautiful cutlery exist today.

He was referring in particular to a number of designs by Luigi Caccia Dominioni and Livio and Pier Giacomo Castiglioni; designs that represent a sort of borderline between the past – the craftmade product – and the future – the industrial manufacture of household goods. The basic pieces of the 'Caccia' cutlery were designed in 1938 and appeared for a year or two on the Italian market in a craftmade version in silver. Thanks to an agreement with the heirs of the Castiglioni brothers and Luigi Caccia Dominioni, it is now being made by Officina Alessi in the silver-plated alpaca version, after a careful philological study of the original design was conducted by Caccia Dominioni himself, who furthermore designed the pieces missing from the original set to complete the 'Caccia' range 50 years after its inception. After many years, and in the light of contemporary industrial reality and the progress of Italian design one thing is now certain, that in the debate of the 1930s and 1940s on the possibility of producing high quality industrial products, these pioneers of 'Lombard classicism' were right in their predictions.

LA TAVOLA DI BABELE

This is the fourth section in the Officina Alessi programme, which began in 1983 with the 'Rosenschale basket', reconstructed from a Josef Hoffmann prototype of 1906 by two young American architects, Peter Arnell and Ted Bickford. This series aims to be an intellectual journey through the history of the mass production of small metal houseware objects. A journey whose stages are objects chosen for their originality, their force and their quality. Unlike the Tea and Coffee Piazza and Archivi series, all the objects of La Tavola di Babele are industrially produced products, often produced at the extreme limits of technical expertise. The authors are Piero Bottoni, Andrea Branzi, Marianne Brandt, Luigi Caccia Dominioni, Achille, Livio and Pier Giacomo Castiglioni, Lluís Clotet, Riccardo Dalisi, Christopher Dresser, Frank Gehry, Josef Hoffmann, Alessandro Mendini, Paolo Portoghesi, Aldo Rossi, Philippe Starck and Robert Venturi.

RIGHT FROM ABOVE: 'Achphat' and 'Tlemcen' candle sticks, Paolo Portoghesi, 1988; cocktail shaker, Marianne Brandt, (1925) 1989; candy bowls, 3-piece set, Piero Bottoni, (1928/29) 1991; OPPOSITE: 'Peyrano' chocolate box, Alessandro Mendini, 1990; PAGES 80-81: 'Dresser Family', Christopher Dresser, round tray and toast rack (1878) 1991, oil and vinegar set (1885) 1993, condiment sets designed by Brian Asquith from Christopher Dresser 1993; PAGE 81 FROM ABOVE: 'Rosenschale' fruit basket, Josef Hoffmann, (1906) 1983; 'The Campidoglio' tray, Robert Venturi, 1985; 'Foix' tray, Luis Potet, 1994

ARCHIVI

Archivi, the fifth section in the Officina series, originated in 1985 with the Tea and Coffee Set with Kettle by Marianne Brandt, followed in 1987 by the Tea Set with Urn by Eliel Saarinen, and in 1991 by a group of objects designed by Christopher Dresser. Its intention, like that of La Tavola di Babele, is to assemble a number of objects which significantly testify to creative moments, historical periods or the work of artists of special interest in the history of the design of small metal objects. Unlike La Tavola di Babele, these designs are characterised by a certain complexity of construction; many of them were conceived for 'noble' metals rather than for mass production, and are thus excellent examples of production by artisan methods. Furthermore, they are in a way curiosities: these designs have never been implemented, or were originally produced only as prototypes.

BACKGROUND IMAGE: Tea Set with Urn, Eliel Saarinen, (1933-34) 1987; INSET FROM ABOVE: Tea and Coffee Service, Marianne Brandt, (1924)

1985; Christopher Dresser collection, (1864-80) 1991

ANTOLOGIA ALESSI

This Anthology series is a review of the most significant articles manufactured by Alessi throughout its history, here reproduced in electro-plated stainless steel. These pieces have been carefully selected for their historical importance, their design validity and their success with the public. They include the bar equipment and trays by Ettore Sottsass, the shaker and the ice bucket by Massoni and Mazzeri, the flatware by Achille Castiglioni and the reissue of the famous Bombé tea and coffee set, designed by Carlo Alessi in 1945.

BELOW: 'Bombé' tea and coffee service, Carlo Alessi Anghini, (1945) 1983

LA CASA DELLA FELICITÀ
THE HOUSE OF HAPPINESS 1980-88

La Casa della Felicità is the first architectural project undertaken by Alessi. It was developed by Alessandro Mendini, Francesco Mendini and Giorgio Gregori (Atelier Alchimia) from 1980-88, with contributions from other architects connected with Alessi: Andrea Branzi (a small outside fountain), Achille Castiglioni (fireplace), Riccardo Dalisi (gables), Frank Gehry (the conservatory), Milton Glaser (railings), Aldo Rossi (tower), Ettore Sottsass (fireplace) and Robert Venturi (library).

The site was a small picturesque area with two old stables situated by Lake Orta . . . between an old Roman and an eighteenth-century road. The intention of the project was to create an ideal shelter which was more an 'intellectual' dwelling than a 'spatial' one; existential and psychological rather than physical. This led to the adoption of a form of 'non-project' approach to create a sensitive shelter free in its style of architecture, ethereal, almost fairy tale-like, expansive, de-concentrated, whereby the intervention of other architects would respond to the clients' needs, with an experimental and literary style. 'To have a non-programmed house, one which, on the contrary, is always unexpected like listening to good music, reading a good book that has a narrative quantity to be discovered a little at a time. . .'

In this sense the Casa della Felicità was intended as a house of happy projects, an authentic project, well conceived, free, strong, a manifesto of a theme very dear to Alessi in these years: an autonomy which is an integral part of the project in its attempt to become a piece of poetry — autonomy arising from the client in the case of the house, or the market place in the case of an industrial project.

La Casa della Felicità was also conceived as an ideal and stimulating place for the experimentation with, and generation of, a collection of furniture accessories from Alessi: a trolley by Enzo Mari, tongs for the fireplace by Pep Bonet, a folding chair and a table lamp by Aldo Rossi, a small table by Ettore Sottsass, a lamp by Alessandro Mendini, fireplace tools by Achille Castiglioni and a barbecue by Stefan Moravez.

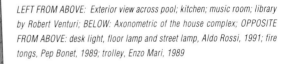

LEFT FROM ABOVE: Exterior view across pool; kitchen; music room; library by Robert Venturi; BELOW: Axonometric of the house complex; OPPOSITE FROM ABOVE: desk light, floor lamp and street lamp, Aldo Rossi, 1991; fire tongs, Pep Bonet, 1989; trolley, Enzo Mari, 1989

MANTEL AND KITCHEN CLOCKS AND 'TIME KEEPER'

MICHAEL GRAVES 1988-92

In designing the mantel clock, I was interested in exploring the well established tradition of seeing artifacts as miniature architecture. There are countless examples where furniture and artifacts stand in interiors as idealised objects which take their primary clues from proportional systems of architecture. I have always been interested in the ambiguity derived between these suggestions for 'interior buildings' and their exterior precedents.

At the same time, I think it is important not to trivialise either, by making interior artifacts as imitation buildings. It is, however, legitimate to express similarities and figurative identities in making interior artifacts relate to the familiar and traditional landscape of architecture itself. We have, therefore, provided proportional divisions in this clock which could be seen as both allegorical and miniaturised versions of a larger architecture.

The pendulum exists in the void provided by the colonnade, while the clock face exists in the space of architecture traditionally reserved for the *piano nobile*. The two figures are then capped appropriately with the head or cornice of the composition. In this way we are able to attain readings of the clock as cabinet, the clock as architecture and finally the clock as clock.   *Michael Graves*

FROM ABOVE: Mantel Clock, 1988; 'Time Keeper', 1992; Kitchen Clock, 1992

CUCKOO CLOCK

ROBERT VENTURI (1986) 1988

Everyone knows what cuckoo clocks are and almost everyone loves them. It was a nice challenge to take what is is at once a familiar form and a vivid symbol and retain its loveable qualities and make it new and fresh at the same time.

We did this by diminishing its hand-craft qualities and abstracting its form, increasing its scale and intensifying its colours . . . this to create a bold kind of image appropriate for our time.   *Robert Venturi*

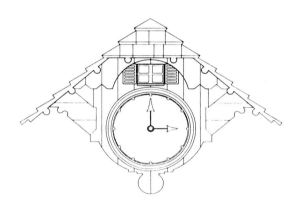

'WALTER WAYLE II'
PHILIPPE STARCK (1988) 1990

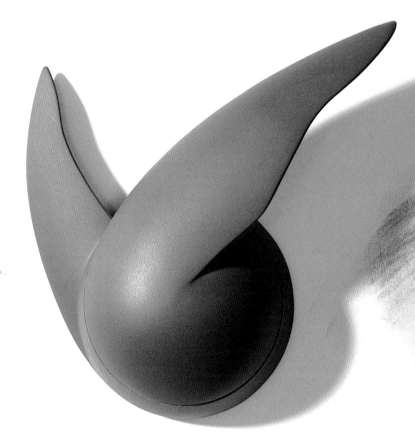

 I like the release of precision. I like clocks, those wide symbols where everyone can roam about and find their own way. The very idea of time is a real drama for me, and alas, I just revel in it.

Working on a clock therefore could only have been fascinating. How on earth could such a small object, made with bits of wood and chewing-gum, contain such a great mystery; how could this window be so effective, and how could it be helped? On such a limited scale myself, I could not enlarge the idea of time. But I could extend the dimension of its earthly representation. So then, let's liberate the hands! Poor things, shut up in a box day and night. Out of pure humanity, I designed railcar hands. They can move by themselves, with no more constraints. Their field of action is immense, infinite. Their references can be at once domestic and cosmic, and they themselves are astonished by this.

After solving the 'moral' problem, I had to find a body for this clock. And so, why not make it with flesh and muscles in view of our probable future, through this osmosis of technology and our flesh which will at last make us similar to God? And I hope He won't prevent it ticking, out of jealousy, but will confine Himself to noting: 'Yet it moves!'
Philippe Starck

'DEAR VERA'
SHIGERU UCHIDA (1989) 1991

As a piece of small architecture, the clock lives amongst us. Separate from big architecture and interiors, its distinct presence makes our lives as distinguished as they ought to be. An object often finds its own place in a room. This clock keeps time on top of a small shelf in our dining room as if it earned its place over a decade. 'Dear Vera' was originally born as an accessory to Hotel 11 Palazzo in Fukuoka, Japan, a building which I created together with the architect Aldo Rossi. The name is borrowed from his daughter.   *Shigeru Uchida*

BACKGROUND IMAGE: 'Dear Vera 2'; INSET: 'Dear Vera 1'

'MOMENTO'
ALDO ROSSI (1986) 1987

 Clocks were at one time the object of study by architects, starting with the meridian, which is associated with the light of the sun, right up to the clocks, which were complicated mechanisms, constructed by Piermarini during his youth. After that, the clock parted company with architecture to become something exclusively technical and a mystery to the layman.

The architect therefore regarded the clock as an element of architecture, in a sense equivalent to the effect of light and shade and, so to speak, a 'concentrate' of the time factor in an architectural design. I have always included clocks in my drawings and structures, especially in public buildings, schools, piazzas and town halls. Time by the clock-tower, so to speak. But the personal wrist or pocket watch that we have on us is something that tells us about the moment: the moment to leave, to begin, to wait, etc. It is a very short space of time, a *temporis punctum*. But unlike the instant, it has no association with speed, but more with quality and quantity . . . [The] intrinsic tension and, at the same time, fragility of the moment is protected by the steel of the watch. Watches cannot be fragile, because they have to mark something that cannot be arrested and is thus capable of untold violence: time.

They must preferably be made of steel, unless we are prepared to contemplate watches made of paper, capable of marking with their own combustion the moments of life. This would be a different, physical concept of the quality of time, as though it were interrupted and sporadic – which it perhaps is – and we only noted anomalies, or stopped at the irregularities that in some way indicate the pathology of time.

But since we cannot pursue this path, we use the well-tried technique of the watch's mechanism as we know it. That is, we defend the recording of continuity. Thus, this familiar watch is, of course, in the majority of cases and for reasons of functionality, round, has Arabic numerals and contains within itself ever more sophisticated instruments, yet, so to speak, has so far concealed them inside a timeless form. But within this perhaps melancholy continuity, we know that the quality of the moment presents a challenge to the obtusely relentless march of time.   *Aldo Rossi*

LEFT: Design sketches and variations of 'Momento' including the 'Momento' wall clock

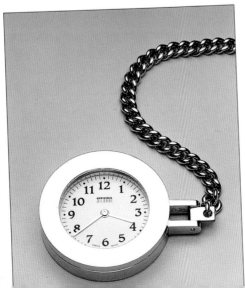

'URI-URI'
RICHARD SAPPER (1987) 1988

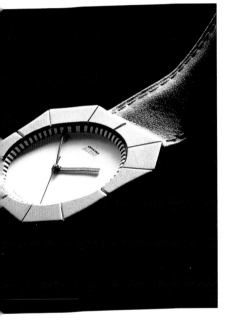

Timepieces have always fascinated me. Tiny machines, complicated but understandable. Precise instruments, useful for everybody because they tell us things we want to know, and if we wear one on our wrist it becomes both jewellery and business card. They have a long history among the oldest machines we know. When a new one is designed, it becomes another link in this chain.

All this was true until about ten years ago when micro-electronics, with one blow, assassinated the jewelled mechanism. It no longer made sense to invent complicated mechanisms or to design watch faces and hands. A chip, a tiny piece of quartz crystal, a liquid crystal display – and the watch without mechanism, without moving parts, with an unheard of precision and an unending number of added functions, from the calculator to the alarm, was created – and all that for a few dollars. The traditional watch, according to any form of logic, is dead. Or is it?

Apparently, it appears not everyone is thinking logically, because slowly, slowly, the traditional watch is making a comeback. Evidently humanity was too comfortable with his old friend. Today we live, as far as watches are concerned, in a 'post-technological' era. An era in which this anachronistic instrument has become a fashion accessory, an object of mass consumption and of 'planned obsolescence'.

Here, I think things are going a little too far, and as far as I'm concerned, I'd like to return to the good old lifetime companion; mini-machine instrument of measurement – jewellery-business card, durable and almost always used – and when it's not, it really doesn't matter because that is usually a notably happier moment in time. *Richard Sapper*

LEFT FROM ABOVE: 'Uri-Uri', colour variations; RIGHT: Design sketch

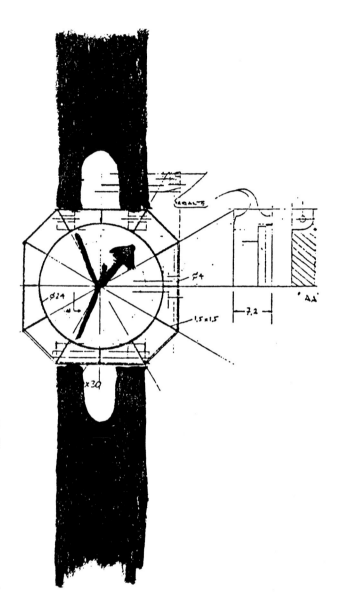

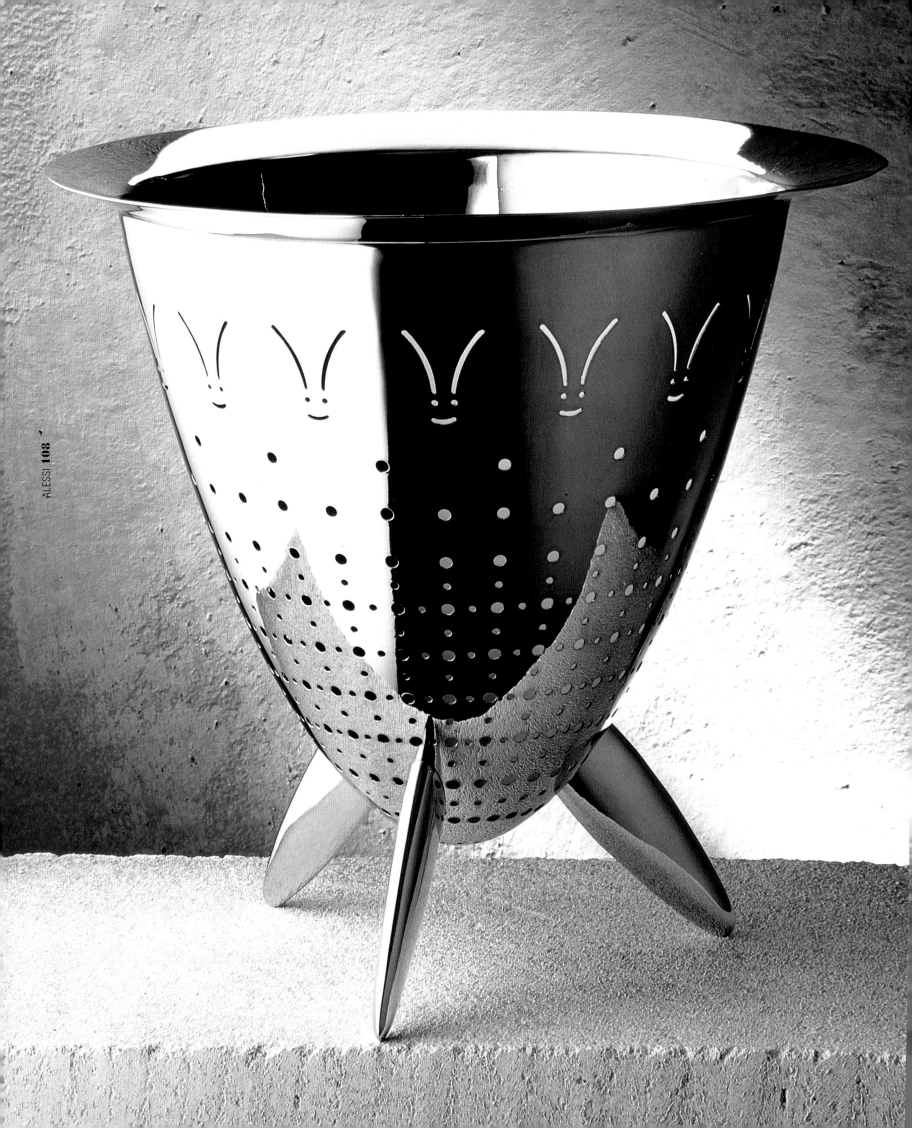

'URI-URI'
RICHARD SAPPER (1987) 1988

Timepieces have always fascinated me. Tiny machines, complicated but understandable. Precise instruments, useful for everybody because they tell us things we want to know, and if we wear one on our wrist it becomes both jewellery and business card. They have a long history among the oldest machines we know. When a new one is designed, it becomes another link in this chain.

All this was true until about ten years ago when micro-electronics, with one blow, assassinated the jewelled mechanism. It no longer made sense to invent complicated mechanisms or to design watch faces and hands. A chip, a tiny piece of quartz crystal, a liquid crystal display – and the watch without mechanism, without moving parts, with an unheard of precision and an unending number of added functions, from the calculator to the alarm, was created – and all that for a few dollars. The traditional watch, according to any form of logic, is dead. Or is it?

Apparently, it appears not everyone is thinking logically, because slowly, slowly, the traditional watch is making a comeback. Evidently humanity was too comfortable with his old friend. Today we live, as far as watches are concerned, in a 'post-technological' era. An era in which this anachronistic instrument has become a fashion accessory, an object of mass consumption and of 'planned obsolescence'.

Here, I think things are going a little too far, and as far as I'm concerned, I'd like to return to the good old lifetime companion; mini-machine instrument of measurement – jewellery-business card, durable and almost always used – and when it's not, it really doesn't matter because that is usually a notably happier moment in time.   *Richard Sapper*

LEFT FROM ABOVE: 'Uri-Uri', colour variations; RIGHT: Design sketch

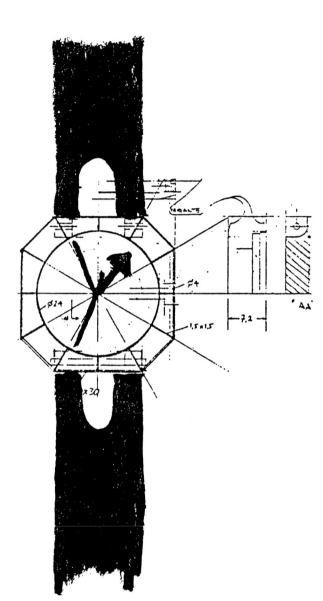

'TEKTON'
MATTEO THUN (1987) 1989

Matteo Thun is a kind of *homo universalis*, forever foreshadowing surprises. An architect by training, he made a name for himself earlier on as a designer of furniture, ceramics and glassware, while at the same time teaching product design at the Hochschule fur angewandte Kunst in Vienna.

He belongs to that new international network of young 'image cultivators' for whom the interchangeability of visual experiences in the various fields of culture engenders a semiotic continuity. Fashion becomes graphics, graphics design, design architecture, architecture cinema. Reality and its interpretation, facts, opinions and phenomena intersect in a continual interplay of parts. Thun grew up under the influence of the new linguistic and semantic theories. Despite his linguistic inheritance which might be defined as Calvinistic-naturalist, he observes with detached amusement its scholastic and mannerist expressions.

We are faced, he says, with a 'semantic chaos' which on the one hand may be realistically accepted, but which on the other needs to be structured.

Like the architects Stirling, Hollein, Isozaki, Tigerman, Graves, Stern or Koolhaas, like the fashion designers Miyake, Lagerfeld, Kenzo or Gaultier, Thun belongs to the category of 'iconographic structuralists'.

He too believes in the force of the image and in the semantic strength of objects. He too belongs to the creative minds of this second modern era. The new opulence of the image, this mixture of forms, colours, textures and structural elements that draw inspiration from all areas of culture from all times, has always fascinated Matteo Thun, in contrast to the stern dullness of the School of Ulm.

A few years ago, Thun drafted a manifesto with the emblematic title 'The Baroque Bauhaus', by which apparently paradoxical term he meant the possibility of enriching abstract and essential forms through work on surface, texture and colour.

The spiritual fathers of this manifesto are not only Kurt Schwitters and Ettore Sottsass, but also and chiefly the French philosophers Lyotard and Foucault.   *Volker Fischer*

'EYE'
MARIO BOTTA

 In the dial space [the watch] describes the passing of time. It is an autonomous architectural object, with its own image, space and workings. It is a microcosm which encloses the fascination of the 'finished' object . . . I had noticed that when one reads the time, one does not look at the date, and vice versa, that they are two distinct functions . . . And so I separated the date indication from that of the time at the centre of the dial, adopting a design for a precise, simple, beautiful and sensual object, and so I called it 'Eye'.   *Mario Botta*

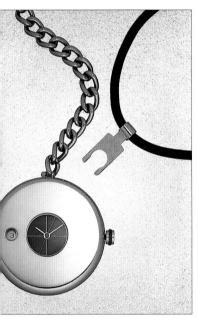

ALESSI **102**

PROJECT SOLFÉRINO AND STARCK
1986

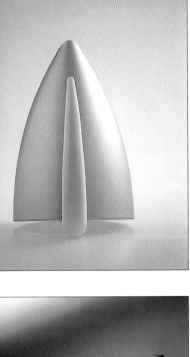

 This project was part of our friendly relationship with Francois Burkhardt, who after the experience at Berlin's IDZ had become chief of the Centre de Création Industrielle at the Beaubourg in Paris.

Towards the mid-eighties, Francois had told me about his interest in organising a large exhibition on Alessi in Paris, and as part of the dealings he sent to Crusinallo the two members of 'Nemo', a French design group of a certain notoriety. Their brief was to explore the feasibility of the Beaubourg's plan for the 'cultural/commercial promotion' of a series of projects concerning French design. As was to be expected, they had many difficulties at home, and Alessi's possible adhesion would have been greatly welcomed. Together with Francois and Alessandro we chose five designers: the 'Nemo's, naturally, and the architects Jean Nouvel, Christian De Portzamparc, Charlotte Perriand and Philippe Starck.

With Danilo, I organised a complete presentation of Alessi for the designers, including commentaries on the production phases of some of our typical products, which took place in the rooms of the Ecole Camondo.

Apart from Starck, none of the other figures were able to come up with interesting results, despite the reciprocal commitment proffered. [Out of all the projects that were elaborated only four articles by Starck were put into production between 1989 and 1990: the kettle 'Haroun Vulcano'; the 'Juicy Salif' lemon squeezer; the 'Max le Chinois' vegetable strainer/washer and the 'Walter Wayle II' wall clock.] That was, for me, a sad acknowledgement of the fact that in France (at least at that moment in history) the conditions for a design useful to Alessi didn't exist. But, after all – even if it could have come about in some other

way – it marked the beginning of the extremely successful collaboration with Philippe.
Extract from Alberto Alessi's Factory Journal

The Projects
The aspect that I found most interesting about Starck's project plans was the closeness of the results of his project methods to those of his artistic creation; for example, the creation of objects that were in a certain sense almost useless when it came to function, objects where at times the function is secondary to the expressive values of the object, such as the sensorial values. Alternatively, 'impracticability' in the sense that it obtains a functional result only through a process of figurative creativity as is found in the case of the fruit juice squeezer designed for the Solférino project.

In the designs for the fruit juice squeezer Starck started designing with its functional aspects only to culminate with an image that looked more like an octopus standing up on three legs, channelled to allow the juice to flow: he worked on an idea that eventually compelled him to design on the basis of the object's functionality.

The kettle has the obliquely styled shape of an Howitzer, as if it was pierced by a conical tube, by an arrow, functioning at one end as a handle into which the water is poured and at the other as a spout for the water to pour out. It has the appearance of a religious object, and the original idea was to have a Latin inscription embossed in ancient lettering.

The vegetable cleaner proved to be an ironic piece of kitchenware ritual: it is wonderful, very big and purely because of its beauty it is expensive, it is heavy and strong in design, unlike any other vegetable cleaner. *Alberto Alessi*

I don't work with Alessi, I work with Alberto Alessi. I don't work with companies, I work with people. I'm only interested in experimenting with the projects and the result is surely secondary.

Alberto Alessi is a great player and that is all that matters to me . . .

Generally when I work on a project I get interested in everything except for the object itself, intuition evolves unexpectedly through work which tends to be detached and parallel to my subconscious. Above all I want my projects to show emotion. In fact I believe that one of our responsibilities is to be able to offer a small piece of poetry of a different moment through an emotion. The cultural side doesn't interest me as much. This emotion is expressed by the means of volumes, colours and materials that become a vector of communication . . .

Today, the only sentiment that I try to rouse with my designs is one of sympathy . . . I try to make use of every aesthetic notion and every cultural notion so that my objects are capable of establishing a bond of fondness (affection) with their users.

Of course it can be done through the medium of poetry, surprises, provocations, mysteries, in whatever discreetly possible way . . .

My projects depend upon the spherical organisation of a multitude of parameters which sometimes become detached from the object itself, yet intuition always remains at its core. At times, for the sake of a more accurate strategy or even from indolence, certain parameters are more domineering than others. Eventually, everything is filtered from a series of exigencies that authenticate the product's originality.

In developing the project, one of the most significant moments is the gestation phase for the draft. Then there is the product elaboration which I do not get involved with. The only moments of a project which interest me are the meetings with my editor where we bashfully talk about other things . . . I am fairly disinterested when it comes to the eventual destiny of my designs since the result of interference by others in this state of intuition cannot offer anything other than surprises and subsequently some form of entertainment. I am ready for anything and everything, even if it means losing the quality of the product, so long as I do not get bored . . .

The component of 'surprise' in a project is an indispensable factor that is measurable around 15 per cent. Below this 15 per cent 'surprise' factor the product will not have that bond of affection with its user because it obviously has nothing new to say or prove and will have less impact in history. Above this percentage we can only assume that there is a risk of misunderstandings or rejection from the user, however, (even though) this represents a real pity for

people whose work ends up being the best way of express-
ing themselves.

I very much like the idea of surprise, it is a sort of mental
short circuit which can generate many other things and
evoke a personal feeling for the user . . .

A designer/architect should be a humanist, he is a
creator, in addition to all the professional or cultural
proposals, which can only act as accessories to emphasise
the point of helping people to live better lives. This can only
come about thanks to his intuition and his fantasy. It's none
other than a service profession where generosity is
obligatory. The nearest other profession would be that of a
missionary . . .   *Philippe Starck, 1989*

*LEFT: 'Hot Bertaa' kettle, 1990-91, stainless steel prototype; PAGE 102: 'Hot
Bertaa', and 'Juicy Salif' lemon squeezer, 1990-91; PAGE 103 FROM ABOVE:
'Hot Bertaa', design sketch; 'Ti Tang' tea pot, 1991-92, Tendentse; 'Voilà-
Voilà' tray, 1992; PAGE 106-07: 'Juicy Salif'; PAGE 108: 'Max le Chinois'
colander, 1990; PAGE 109: 'Mister Meumeu' parmesan cheese cellar and
grater, 1992*

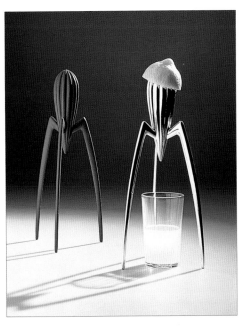

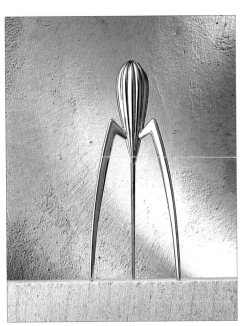

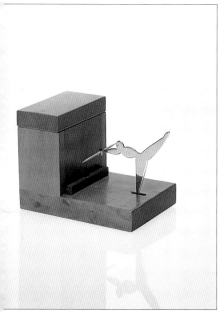

TWERGI

1988-

In 1988 the idea of marketing wooden objects evolved. A chance meeting with one of the heirs of Battista Piazza, a company established in 1865, eventually brought about the opportunity to make objects from wood. This ancient company, situated in the Strona Valley by Lake Orta, specialised in making small wooden table and kitchenware objects using wood turning methods, but had ceased operating twenty years earlier.

The Strona Valley is a poor area where even today entire families still survive working with wood. Almost all wooden spoons are made there. It is a craftsmanship completely immersed in a medieval culture, an interesting production and tradition that has stood still in time and quality.

It was decided that Alessi would work with the company to help make quality improvements using a wide variety of woods – ebony, rose, pear, apple, cherry, olive, beech, ash, alder, lime, brier, our own walnut, acacia and birch – while still maintaining the same production methods

> The craftsmanship of wood turning has always fascinated me, even before I discovered that my ancestors were from the Strona Valley and worked as wood turners . . . I also believe that to stop and rethink this production method could provide valuable help for a new progressive solution to our own 'sophisticated' technology. Maybe, even our method of designing.

The Twergi programme is an initiative destined to develop in a highly competitive Italian and European market. Over the years Alessi has managed to develop and implement an engineering capacity for complex design processes. This involves having a close association with many high profile designers all over the world and in having established a team of professionals within the company capable of dealing with diverse production problems and in developing the company's activities that are not part of Alessi's original production, such as the use of wood.

Twergi was the first opportunity which allowed the Alessi metaproject programme to constitute a new small and independent business while remaining connected to its general development strategy. Sottsass and certain other designers who work or have worked in his studio – Marco Zanini, Aldo Cibic, James Irvine, Adalberto Pironi, Mike Ryan, Massimo Iosa Ghini – and Milton Glaser from New York, all collaborated in this operation.

Some of the projects together with the graphic designs were entrusted to Sottsass. Milton Glaser, (who is also an expert in gastronomy) was asked to design a series of chopping boards and the logo type of the series. Glaser's collaboration appeared intriguing and interesting; an American graphic designer, he was even asked to design the 'Twergi' despite the fact that he knew nothing about the Strona Valley. The idea for the logo came from the original Battista Piazza company's first trademark, the 'Twergi'. The twergi were elfs, creatures of popular myth who lived in the mountain woods. Milton Glaser modified the Piazza trademark, giving Alessi's twergi skis on his feet.

From the typological point of view research was divided into five sections: the chopping boards; the condiment set; the oil containers and the bowls; the mill sets; the trays and kitchen utensils – plates for risotto etc . . . The operation was coordinated by Alberto Alessi and Davide Piazza with research by Marco Zanini and Mike Ryan supervised by Sottsass.

The first new catalogue was published in 1989. There were some original items that formed part of the old catalogues by Piazza: two pepper mills from 1919 and 1946, a coffee grinder dating back to 1930 and a cheese grater of 1912. A year on from its establishment it was necessary to give this operation a consistent and complete metaproject to adapt the Twergi range to the ambitious programme of Alessi and wood.   *Laura Polinoro*

RIGHT: Sketches for: salad bowl, Massimo Iosa-Ghini; the Twergi trademark, Milton Glaser; pepper mill, Massimo Iosa-Ghini; pepper mill, Massimo Iosa Ghini, 1988; pepper mill, James Irvine, 1989; OPPOSITE FROM ABOVE L TO R: Pear toothpick holder, Andrea Branzi, 1992; alder salad bowl and bowl, Massimo Iosa-Ghini, 1989; aniline coloured beech condiment set, Ettore Sottsass, 1989; pear salt mill, 1992, toothpick holder, 1994, pepper mill, 1991, and chilli mill, 1992, Andrea Branzi; walnut and metal ring holder, Andrea Branzi, 1994; kawazingo and ash pepper mill, Massimo Iosa-Ghini, 1989; cherry and aluminium personal mirror, Ico Migliore and Mara

Servetto, 1992; aniline coloured beech cork screws, 1993, pepper mill, 1989, and egg cup, 1993, Ettore Sottsass; brass and douglas-wood coffee mill, Riccardo Dalisi, 1990; PAGES 112-13 BACKGROUND IMAGE: Round melamine trays, King Kong, 1993; INSET: hand painted wooden boxes, image by Nuala Goodman, form by James Howett, 1994 (Memory containers); coloured beech condiment set, salt and pepper castor set and coloured lime wood parmesan cheese cellar, Alessio Pozzoli and Sam Ribet, 1993; storage jars with coloured beech tops, Ettore Sottsass, 1994; coloured wooden place marker, King Kong, 1990

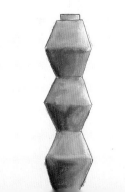

TENDENTSE
1989

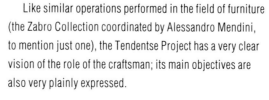

Project for a Revival of the Artisan Tradition

The Tendentse Project was born in 1985: its objective was to generate experimental research aimed at production. From the very beginning the project was conceived as a way of reviving and giving new life to the artisan tradition. The medium chosen was ceramics. Precisely because its origins are so ancient, the art of pottery can benefit from a revision of the techniques and theories of expression it is based on, as well as a revaluation of its historic heritage in terms of design and production.

The idea of a collection of objects that could function as a barometer and showcase for current trends and probable future tendencies was not worked out in theoretical terms alone: it developed gradually as a result of the contributions of various artists. Starting with the original group of artists, Ettore Sottsass, Adolfo Natalini, Andrea Branzi and Alessandro Mendini, it gradually expanded to include designers of the younger generation, artists representing the most significant and innovative tendencies.

The idea is based on the theory (or rather on the analytical forecast) that in the near future the manufacture of household items will develop along two major lines. On the one hand, the 'informatic' object, a high-tech, hyper-specialised, strictly functional, mass-produced, technically perfect and essentially industrial object. On the other, the craftsman's produce, a handmade object with a powerful emotional content, in which the main qualities and distinguishing features are variability, personalisation and even error, all the direct result of the artist's personal manual involvement.

The idea is that this sphere of production, thanks to its flexibility and lack of technical and manufacturing limitations, will provide a fertile area for experimentation, the results of which will be useful for industrial production as well. It is seen as a sort of factory of projects and ideas that will provide new lifeblood not necessarily to the traditional artisan sector alone.

Like similar operations performed in the field of furniture (the Zabro Collection coordinated by Alessandro Mendini, to mention just one), the Tendentse Project has a very clear vision of the role of the craftsman; its main objectives are also very plainly expressed.

First of all, since the Utopian myth of mass production and industrial reproducibility has crumbled, their intention is to stress the importance of manual intervention, of the quality of difference, of the value of objects that are never exactly the same as any other: in other words, their aim is to re-evaluate those characteristics that mass production, for industrial reasons, had eliminated.

Secondly, it is their intention to rediscover the extraordinary historical heritage of the artisan tradition, of methods and types of craft production that are gradually dying out, of the expertise acquired and consolidated over centuries of technical development.

In the last 30 years artisan production has capitulated to industrial production, which seems to have absorbed all the innovative ideas and designs. From an aesthetic point of view artisan products appear to have exhausted their creativity. Stuck in the rut of obsolete formal stereotypes that are repeated almost mechanically artisan ceramic, wood, metal and textile production has for the most part degenerated into kitsch.

The aim of this project for the revival of the artisan tradition is to step out of this stagnant, negative historical phase, creating objects that are original and innovative from the design stage through to the manufacturing process.

The project's trump card is that it will set in motion a circular process in which the creative ability of the designers, the nature of materials, the mastery of technique and the manual execution will all interact in a unitary and compact way to make a quality product.

Drawing up unprecedented formal codes, the Tendentse collection proposes a new, delicate, non-aggressive, colourfully classical language, which will generate the artisan tradition of the future.

Following a procedure which we might call post-industrial, this neo-artisan tradition is potentially an excellent indicator of new trends, for it will keep us informed as to the current and developing tendencies in the field of artistic expression.   *Patrizia Scarzella*

In 1989 the tradename and catalogue 'Tendentse' were acquired by Officina Alessi and after their relaunch in 1990 became the second new episode in the adventures of Alessi after Twergi.

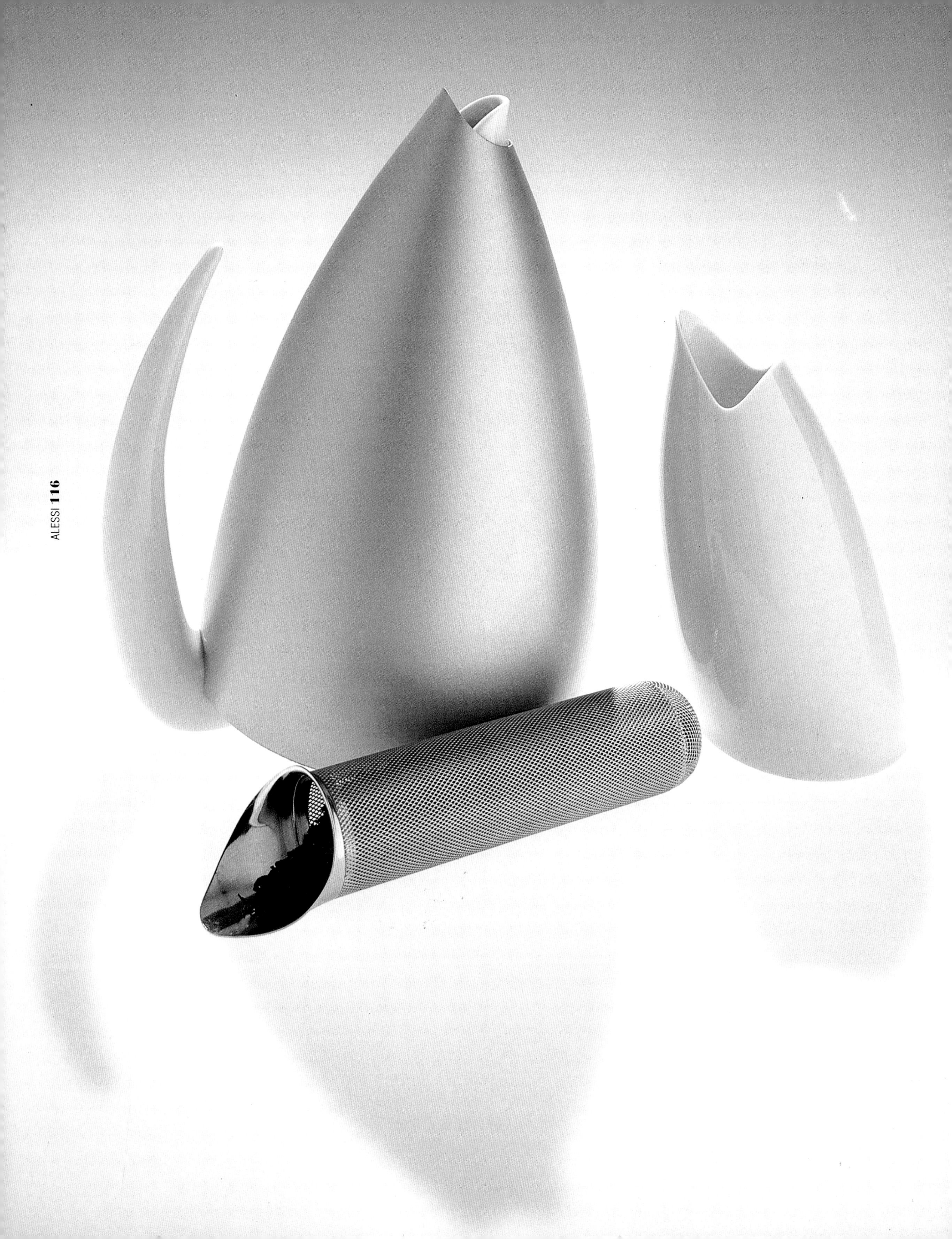

signal that would immediately appeal to the memory or, in other words, a sort of archetypal communications culture. This was the concept behind all the FFF series objects introduced in 1993.

The chain of little men is the same motif that children make with paper cut-outs. The idea was to treat stainless steel as if it were paper, having the little men circling the edge as if they were holding hands and keeping together the objects in the bowl with their own 'girotondo'[1].

The introduction of plastic in the egg cup in this otherwise purely metal range, was of a practical nature, since with its pliable nature it accommodates a wide range of egg sizes.

The punch reflects the serial quality of the project which in turn leads to the popcorn machine and fast-food idea as well as to the sound of a pinball machine.

The project was conceived in 1988 and went into production in 1989, an extended range of products is to be released in 1994.

Stefano Giovanni and Guido Venturini, November 1993

1 *Girotondo* is an Italian nursery rhyme, similar in its movements to the English *Ring a Ring a Roses*

BACKGROUND IMAGE: Sets of two stainless steel egg cups with thermo-plastic rubber egg holders, 1991-94; INSET FROM ABOVE: Napkin rings, 1994; tray with pierced edge, 1989-90, and tray with ebonised and aluminium tray handle, Frog Design, 1991; breadstick holder, 1993; round tray with ebonised and aluminium handle; pierced round baskets and fruit basket, 1993, round tray with pierced edge and egg cups

CENTRO STUDI ALESSI

1991-

 After the initial experience of the book *l'Officina Alessi* in July 1989, Alberto Alessi and Alessandro Mendini spoke to me about their idea of creating a research and study centre, a kind of creative forge to integrate and innovate the well tried project system which for many years has characterised the Alessi company of Crusinallo.

The project was undoubtedly complex and at the forefront were a series of theoretical and logistical problems. In the light of past experience the first questions an Alessi Research Centre would have to ask were: What is the job/role of an object? What is it that changes in their form, in the perception we have of them and in their use? How does an object become a cultural subject?

We began a first series of meetings with Paolo Fabbri (semiologist and lecturer in the theory of forms at DAMS in Bologna), Franco La Cecla (researcher at DAMS), Lucetta Scaraffia (researcher at the Institute of Modern History in Rome) and Massimo Alvito (researcher at L'Ecole de Hautes Etudes in Paris), to discuss a number of themes related to the birth, identity and role of objects. We pinpointed a number of areas for research. On the one hand, the transformation in types of table in the West, to be looked at by Lucetta who would try to bring out aspects of the symbolic function of the table. On the other, Franco La Cecla conducted a deeper investigation into the theme of creolisation evident in the purely pragmatic/inter-subjective relationship in object/fetish, while Massimo Alvito looked at the individuation of the object in Japanese culture which is constantly in touch with its invisible world. From these researches developed Memory Containers, the first Centro Studi Alessi project.
Laura Polinoro

'Ovo' kitchen container, Joanna Lyle, Memory Containers, 1994

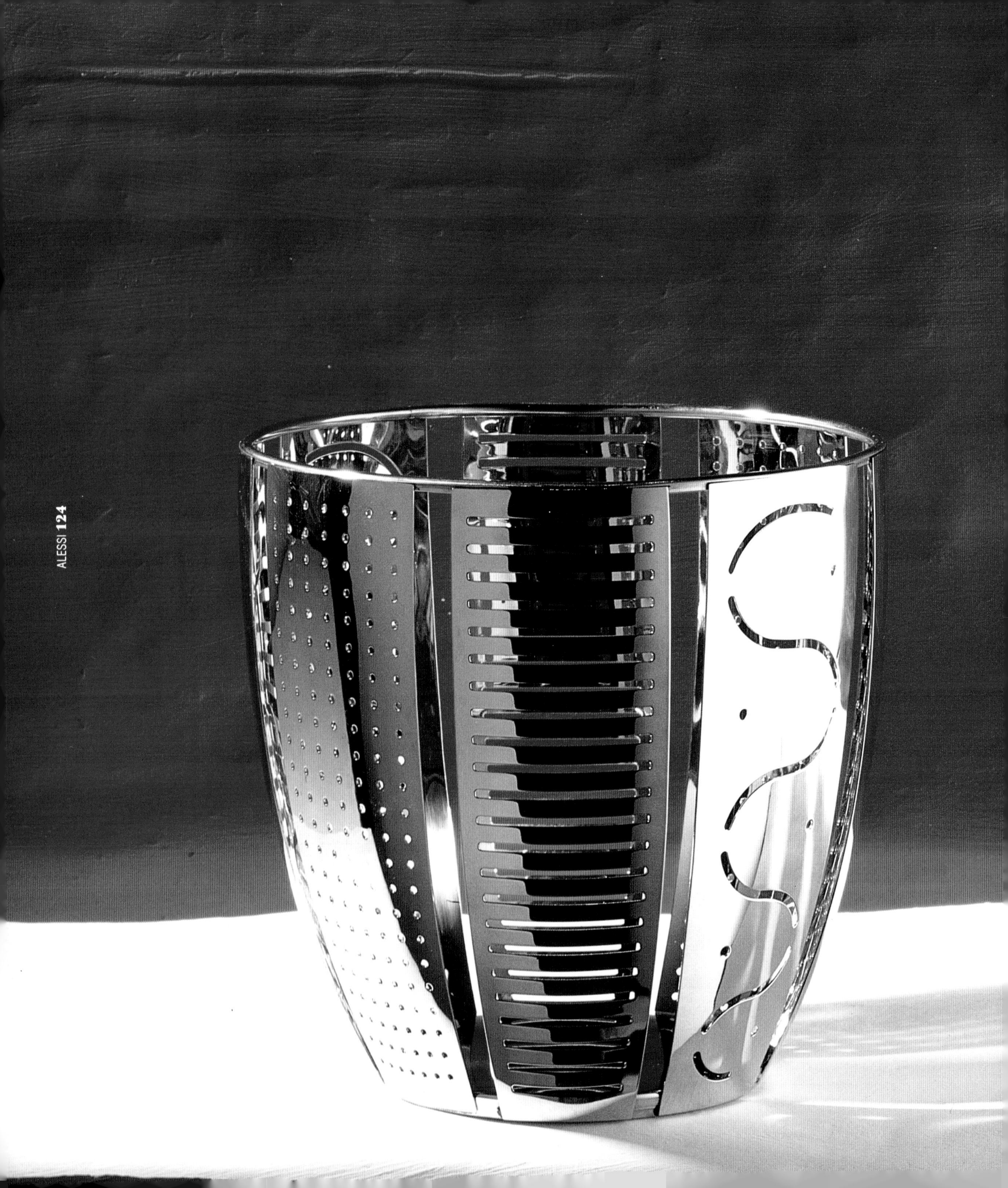

La Bella Tavola and My Beautiful China

Preparing a beautiful table for eating with the family or for eating with friends or because you're engaged or even because you're lovers, is a practised custom and it seems to me a very graceful way of showing awareness, respect and care about that 'basic' event (as the Americans say) of having food.

If there is a beautiful table where everything is neat and tidy, where everything's clean and all the tableware is carefully laid in its proper places, you feel more like taking part in a ritual; perhaps you concentrate better, perhaps you feel a keener psychic and cultural possession of the event as it unfolds, perhaps you become more aware of your luck or even, on occasion, you may even grow aware of participating in a strange, inexplicable cosmic sacrifice. Harmless animals are slain, infinite numbers of fish are fished, infinite quantities of herbs and leaves are cut, water is drawn from the earth, and unknown salts; and the planet, wandering with slow stupidity in a dark sky, is being used up.

A beautiful table is not necessarily a rich table, an expensive one, a nice table is not necessarily pompous, insolent or aggressive, and a beautiful table is not necessarily the poor man's table, I mean a table distracted by the anxiety of poverty.

I think it's very difficult to design a beautiful table; it doesn't depend only on the design of the implements used on it, but on a subtle, frail, uncertain wisdom with which a few people sometimes, heaven knows how and why, succeed in steering into the project to create an event for the total perception of our cosmic adventure: however provisional, suspended and incomprehensible it may be.

Certainly the designing of utensils to be used for organising a beautiful table is important; it's important because even the design of tableware can somehow slow down or accelerate the intensity of the ritual, retard or speed up people's slow, suspicious approach to the perception of existence as an unbearably complicated event.

For this reason I believe it must have been difficult, in ancient times, to design jade discs for Chinese rituals that we don't even know anything about; difficult to design chalices of tender, absolutely pure gold, to gain possession of Christian blood; difficult to design perfect bronzes for Tantric pujas; difficult to design ceramics for Japanese green teas and for that matter I think it is difficult today, too, to design utensils for contemporary rituals, difficult to design blue Suzuki motorbikes to penetrate the border between life and death at 300 kilometres an hour, and difficult also, to design silver utensils for sinking into that speechless space; the horribly silent space.

The rituals of a beautiful table do not aim perhaps so far. I know well that the rituals of a beautiful table are corrupted by the presence of perfumes, tastes, thicknesses, hardness and tenderness, corrupted by the arrival of breezes of unknown origin, by the colours of the seasons, corrupted by lights in the sky . . . I know well that the rituals of the table do not envisage or invoke the presence of perfection, they do not pursue programmes of the spirit, metaphysical yearnings. I know well that the rituals of the table have to do with a gothic presence of the senses, but perhaps it is precisely the complicated, anxious, irreplaceable presence of the senses that we are concerned about. Perhaps we are concerned to explain it, to put it somewhere, on some pedestal, maybe even just to enjoy it and maybe that's why we try to design a few special utensils: even if they are just wooden bowls and occasionally baskets, or hefty drinking glasses or sonorous crystal glasses, large trays, saltcellars and pepper-grinders; and perhaps we may even use only the leaves of a fig or banana tree, and then design celestial silver fruit-stands, or even round plates in thin porcelain . . .

It was thin porcelain plates that I found myself designing this time for Alberto Alessi, for the Alessi company. Let's hope they'll be all right.   *Ettore Sottsass*

RIGHT FROM ABOVE: 'Uomo felice' vase, Ugo Marano, 1990; 'Diavoletti da tavola', Riccardo Dalisi, 1990; OPPOSITE: 'Ti Tang' teapot with stainless steel filter and 'Su-Mi Tang' creamer-sugar bowl, Philippe Starck, 1992; PAGE 114 FROM ABOVE: Decorative panel, Alessandro Mendini, 1985; 'Feoia' fruit bowl, Andrea Nannetti, 1985; 'Cro' vase, Anna Bili, 1985; 'Tatzona', 'Tatzine' and 'Portacondim' condiment set, Andrea Branzi, 1986- *87; 'Maschera', Shama and Tarshito, 1987; 'Superdiscolo' Michele De Lucchi, 1986; 'Colpo di vento', Franco Raggi, 1985; PAGE 115 BACKGROUND IMAGE: Plates from 'La Bella Tavola' and 'My Beautiful China', Ettore Sottsass, 1993, and 'La Bella Tavola and Tutto' Ettore Sottsass, decorated by Alighiero Boetti, 1994; INSET ABOVE: 'La Bella Tavola and My Beautiful China'; BELOW 'La Bella Tavola and Tutto'*

FORMA
SENZA
DECORI

DECORI
VAGANTI

ORNAMENTI

ASTRATTI
INFORMALI
GEOMETRICI
DESCRITTIVI — (RACCONTI)

NATURALISTI
LETTERARI
POPOLARI   NAIF
POP
STORICI
INFANTILI
DEI PAZZI

COLTI
FOLK

ALESSI **118**

ALESSI
TENDENTSE
100%
00001/10.000

MADE IN GERMANY
1992

THE '100% MAKE-UP'
(1989-92)

The project consists of a white porcelain vase produced in ten thousand units [designed by Mendini]. The shape of every vase is the same. Its white body is thought of as a surface on which numerous different signs can be painted.

One hundred decorators were chosen from different anthropological backgrounds: artists, architects, designers and others, from Europe, Asia, Africa and America. Each was asked to decorate the surface of the vase: one hundred vases for one hundred decorators, each in one hundred copies, all at the same price. A choral work. A parade of the ten thousand pieces considered in their entirety: the staging of a performance. A new exploration of the pure, ancient and infinite world of porcelain vases. A synthetic work as a whole, it is, however, also a constellation of visual stories, personal murmurs and shouts. The anonymous hegemony of the series disintegrated and re-composed in a hundred single stories. Just as happens today with the world's political image: a kaleidoscope whose global figures make sense only when the smallest and most decentralised elements express their identity.

Stamped on the base of every vase are the names of all 100 decorators, in alphabetical order, and a number from one to 10,000. The identity of each decorator is indirect but is explained by the numerical sequence. This is for the second phase of the project, when public demand had shown a preference for vases by particular decorators. These vases were reissued in an unlimited, unnumbered edition, and sold at a higher price than that of the original 10,000 for the '100% make-up' operation.

Species not Series

What we had in mind was a system of objects similar to that of a natural species. An aesthetic industrial system bears a certain resemblance to a biological organism: in its pulsation, mechanism, materials, colours and the markings on its skin. A futuristic industrial design project can be conducted on the invention of a limited experiment starting from scratch, as in that of a species.

In fact the species is a large grouping of similar organisms which produces a fecund inheritance through interbreeding: in our case a world run by internal rules, a system of structurally similar but all identifiable and different objects, with an inner logic of reproduction. Assimilation to nature and penetration of nature, where what matters, together with the meaning of single individuals, is the compactness of their cosmos intended as a puzzle.

The Aesthetic Factory

The idea in mind is that of an aesthetic factory. There the production of pieces is treated as the multiplication of their soul, a sequence of original and similar aesthetic creatures, not of repeated technical copies. A design can be conceived to attain the different from the identical. Think of an industrial series (species) in the entirety of its global and conclusive number of pieces. Seen in its final totality, the development of a series is an unattainable and conceptual figure, a cabalistic rhythm, an immobile representation: submitted as an overall general artwork bound to be dissolved when every constitutive element is elsewhere. In the abstract the large dissolved system could afterwards refer back to its own wholeness, and the 10,000 solitary elements be led back to the compactness of their cosmos.

Why a Vase?

A vase has been taken as the leading actor in this operation. The vase is still made of earth; it is elementary in its use and easy to make. It is one of mankind's most ancestral wares. The vase is a repertory and container of legend and rites. It is made on a potter's wheel, one of the most ancient tools in existence. It derives from the shape of a flower and from hands joined together to drink or to offer. Often it contains flowers.

Ornament as Identity

Ornaments today form an ethnic and widespread activity, developing as the transmission of inner feelings, a subject-ive idiom and transmission of dreams, anxieties and myths.

Ornament is painting: flowing without beginning or end through history, and transmitting with its original expres-sions the inexhaustible writing, the subtle vibration of human minds. The decorations are like fishes in the sea: existing even if unseen.   *Alessandro Mendini*

LEFT FROM ABOVE: Mendini's sketches for the development of the vases; information appearing on the base of the first series of vases; vase by Mara Voce; OPPOSITE LEFT: Sketches by Mendini; OPPOSITE FROM ABOVE L TO R: Vases selected for the second phase of unlimited, unnumbered

production: Alessandro Mendini; Alighiero Boetti; Riccardo Dalisi; Nicola De Maria; Milton Glaser; Michael Graves; Aussi Jaffari; Shiro Kuramata; Mark Kostabi; Kamba Luesa; Sybilla; Robert Venturi

GIROTONDO
KING KONG – STEFANO GIOVANNI AND GUIDO VENTURINI (1989-93)

 Founder members of the Boldist movement, Stefano Giovanni (La Spezia, 1954) and Guido Venturini (Alfonzine, 1957) graduated in architecture in Florence. They work and live in Milan. Since 1979 they have taught and carried out research at Florence Faculty of Architecture; now also at the Domus Academy in Milan. In 1985 they set up King Kong Production, concerning themselves with avant-garde researches in design, interiors, fashion and architecture. Their interest is focused on cartoons, science fiction, celluloid mythology, areas of the imaginary and artificial fiction. They work on the idea as an iconographic, primary and conceptual datum with a mixture of poetry and irony that supersedes the disciplinary conceptions of object form, composition and design.

The original plan for the Girotondo series for Alessi called for a series of objects decorated with a chain of human cut-outs. These plans eliminated or, better still, reduced the formal design of the object to a bare minimum, with everything hinged on the serial repetition of an iconographic and figurative element that everyone could recognise. The little man was the result of our search for a strong figurative

MEMORY CONTAINERS

1991-94

It was decided that concomitant with the research to be carried out by the Centro Studi, a project would be created within the Centre working with young designers, something that the company had never done before. Initially we were not looking for finished projects but for inspiration and ideas that would lead to an actual project. This project would subsequently be developed within the Centre with the help of a team from the company including Alberto Alessi, who would give the company's overall evaluation of the project, Danilo Alliata, who would oversee technical aspects regarding the project's realisation and me, who would take care of the organisational aspects of the operation. In terms of the type of project we were looking for the brief made reference to the architypes of 'the offering' of food and the rituals surrounding it. Inspiration could be drawn from a cultural heritage or from personal experience. The 'objective' was the realisation of a 'creole project', a cloning *in vitro* of something that, left to its own devices, would emerge, if at all, much more slowly as the result of the meeting of disparate cultures. Each designer was aware of the company's overall project but was not told about the 'objective' I had set. What I was initially trying to do was to lift the whole project experience onto a more adventurous level. What I asked the designers to do was to abandon, as far as possible, the stylistic languages they had already absorbed. The condition under which we would work would be one of openness, so as to ensure a greater level of spontaneity in the project's development. It would be sufficient to choose a number of evocative elements which would serve as inspiration for a possible project but which also left enough space to play with the other project variables: namely, the object's real use, both practical and symbolic; how it creates and means a symbolic space indicating an interdependent relationship in social and cultural contexts; and the production and image considerations of Alessi (the possible Alessi). This was the Centre's first approach to working on a project, a project, furthermore, which is defined but is constantly being redefined as work proceeds, playing with already existing company parameters which, rather than being simply endured, need to become so familiar that their integration with new working methods facilitates the development of a more open and flexible creative procedure. *Laura Polinoro*

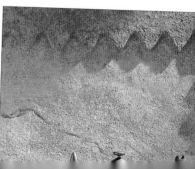

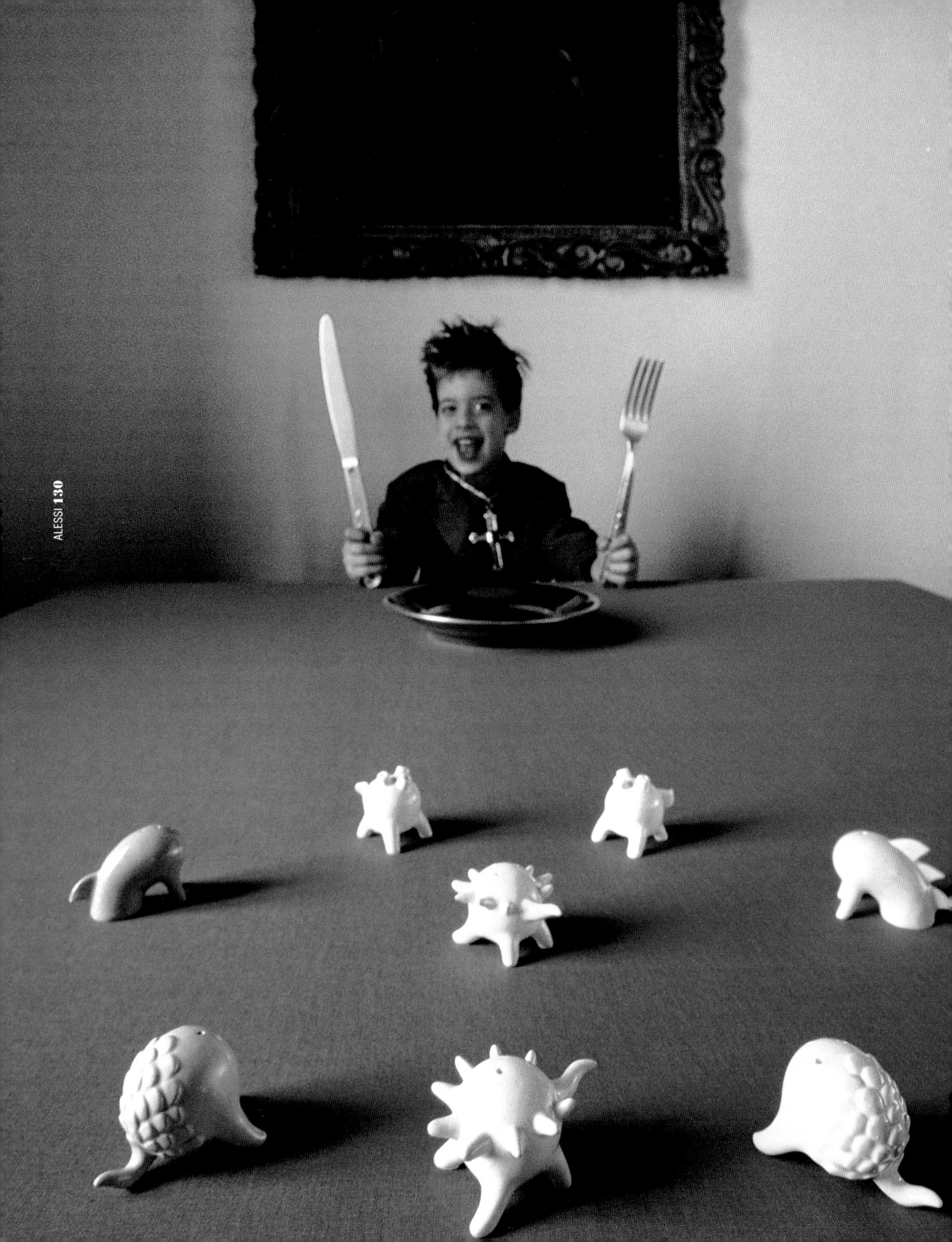

FAMILY FOLLOWS FICTION
1991/1993

Prompted by a number of consultants as well as by our own curiosity, we felt the urgent need for an operation that would attempt to balance the authoritativeness, expressive impact and culturalisation of the projects developed for us by the 'great masters' in the 1980s. This would be done by introducing a more empathic, affective and confidential note into our catalogue. Of course, it was not my intention to stand in any way aloof from those designs of the eighties, indeed we are still working with great passion in that direction, which is central to Alessi's identity. Nor did I intend to look at any cost for novelty for novelty's sake. I simply wanted to make our catalogue richer and more balanced. My intention, therefore, was to explore more explicitly and directly a number of expressive keys, such as play, memory and emotive involvement, that were certainly already present, though in a more hidden form, in the works of those designers.   *Alberto Alessi*

The Workshop: Centro Studi Alessi

This workshop started in February 1991 and, after talks and reflections with Alberto Alessi, Luca Vercelloni and Marco Migliari, a project task support pamphlet was prepared and implemented in April 1991, with Pierangelo Caramia, Stefano Giovannoni, Massimo Morozzi, Giovanni Lauda, Alejandro Ruiz, Denis Santachiara and Guido Venturini . . .

We all had the sensation that there was still a hidden side to the Alessi planet. The authoritativeness, lucidity and impact of the products that had been made until then did not quite satisfy our most delicate, tender, intimate and affective demands. We needed new sensorial experiences, and new materials to represent our new thoughts.

Furthermore, we were aware of being at the end of the millennium, at the end of the 1980s, and perhaps even of having come to the end of the word 'design' as it had been used up until then. We felt the need to shake off our parameters, to think futuristically, released from style and idiom, to throw ourselves into the fascinating and seductive idea of the new century.

Reflection on Franco Fornari's theory of affective codes and Winnicott's writings on transitional objects and paradoxical thinking, provided us with further timely instruments of analysis.

At last the route to be followed by the new workshop became clear – that of the 'object-toy'. And it would be conceived beyond aesthetics, style or culture. 'In a room full of objects a child chooses one to relieve his boredom and solitude; why that object in particular?'

The challenge was to reproduce in terms of design the animistic process of an object, common to the world of representation among children and primitive cultures. The process in any case occurs in the reality of all objects, and is spontaneously triggered by personal, or collective, emotive necessities and by the image-impact of the object itself.

We wanted to discover other materials – plastic, for example – in order better to explore the world of colour and the sensorial dimension of objects.

In the choice of designers, too, this desire for communicative force was taken into account.

The outcome was very interesting: a new chapter in the Alessi world. Perhaps more autonomous products were born, with the capacity to relate independently to the world whilst alluding to known realms of the imagination or, in other cases, to fantastic worlds. Creatures were born. All this truly shows that transformism is possible, and that it is possible to redesign life in this way, beginning with everyday things. It is possible to transform objects, it is possible to be transformed by them, and it is possible to give paradoxical answers without worry. It was a happy project and we can say we enjoyed ourselves.

Between Doing and Playing

It is true that objects must do things, this being the 'objective' criterion that justifies their existence and, of course, it is easy to establish an objective criterion for their usefulness. 'Doing' is one criterion and only one, and it is shared by all.

But in addition to the one-way instrumental subject-object relationship, there exists that of communication; and of knowing about an object in the world where, conversely, it is the object that affects the subject. Now this is certainly the dimension which we at Alessi are most interested in.

A cultural knowledge of objects enables us to recognise them as belonging to a culture, as being related to history and other cultures (a subject we developed in our previous operation and described in the book *Rebus sic*). Besides this, however, we are at present interested in observing how objects indicate and tell a story of doing, of doing something for themselves and for somebody; but also in how they tell a story of relationships. So we wanted to highlight their affective impact, by projecting a situation and a world where objects act and create a sentimental quality whereby they are made desirable, tender and inseparable.

In a society where individual recognisability is linked to production-demand, objects become the new vehicles of an imagery, with the capacity to create new 'families' and consumer identities on the market, new places of recognisability and belonging; the capacity to build not only a sociocultural dimension, but the more intimate dimension of our identity as consumers.

This operation discovers the object transformed into an instrument of play. It tells short fables and gives endearing answers to how that object can be commonly used; suggesting indirect links with play, and stimulating transposition into the fantastic.

'Play', as a tacit agreement allowing the construction of an imaginary world in which we can recognise ourselves, protects our innermost tenderness and creativity, finding a way of sharing it.

If objects are the new vehicles of imagination, their imagery in turn will become, in the world of communication and expression, new vehicles for a confidently creative relationship and easing of tension.   *Laura Polinoro*

ALESSI **132**

BACKGROUND IMAGE: 'Merdolino' toilet brush in thermoplastic resin, Stefano Giovannoni, 1993; INSET FROM ABOVE: Design sketches for: 'Mix Italia' espresso coffee maker, King Kong; 'Gino Zucchino'; 'Merdolino'; PAGE 130: 'Gli Unnini' personal salt and pepper castors, Alejandro Ruiz, 1993 (Tendentse); PAGE 131 FROM ABOVE: 'Lilliput' magnetic salt and pepper set, Stefano Giovannoni, 1993; 'Fruit Mama' fruit holder with green polyamide tree, Stefano Giovannoni, 1993; 'Firebird' electronic gas lighter, Guido Venturini, 1993; 'Stappo' plastic bottle-opener with magnetic stainless steel opener, Massimo Morozzi, 1993; 'Gino Zucchino' plastic sugar sifter, Guido Venturini, 1993; 'Penguin Tea', teapot, Pierangelo Caramia, 1993; 'Nutty the cracker', nutcracker and bowl in aluminium casting and polyamide, Stefano Giovannoni, 1993; PAGE 134 FROM ABOVE L TO R: 'Christy' conical multipurpose sugar bowl with feet in thermoplastic resin, design by Christopher Dresser (1864), colours by Centro Studi, 1993; 'Gino Zucchino'; 'Escar-
_____, Stefano Giovannoni, 1994; 'Diabolix
_____ stainless steel opener, Biagio Cisotti,
_____akers, creamer and sugar bowl, King
_____ E L TO R: 'Firebird', 'Stappo' PG bottle
_____ Massimo Morozzi, 1993; 'Lilliput', 'Nutty
_____ 'Egg' infuser and 'Penguin' pitcher.

ALESSOFONO

1993

 The design of a new saxophone in 1989 . . . has clear historical, methodological and, I might even say, philosophical roots.

The first is a sentimental reason: the Alessofono is a tribute to Grandpa Giovanni, Alessi's founder. In the twenties and thirties his workshop not only produced the table settings and kitchen implements we all know so well, but also participated in the bustling local tradition of producing saxophones [with the local saxophone manufacturer, Rampone & Cazzoni, from the village of Quarna] . . . My grandfather's role was to produce saxophone keys, the instrument's silver and gold coating and the decorative engravings . . .

Another reason has to do with the manufacturing technology: saxophones . . . have the same technical hand crafting roots as household tools and require the same types of metals and manufacturing tools: brass, nickel and silver; the lathe, smelting, small presses and cutters and lots of intricate filing work.

Yet another reason is tied to methodology and consists of the attempt to apply high design to the saxophone. It is our opinion (mine and that of Alessandro Mendini) that when this instrument was invented, over a century ago, Mr Sax focused all his care and genius on the musical aspects of the instruments at the expense of both the ergonomic and aesthetic aspects. And all future saxophone manufacturers followed in his footsteps. Thanks to the encouragement of Davide Mosconi, a musical researcher called in by Mendini for assistance, and of Luca Di Volo, a concert performer and Wind Department co-ordinator from the Fiesole School of Music, responsible for the mechanical improvements to our instrument, we instead believed that the aesthetic and ergonomic aspects could have been improved by adopting a better design logic (Di Volo told us from the very beginning: 'You can't imagine how difficult it is for kids to begin to play the instrument. What we need to do is totally revolutionise the situation and try to bring the instrument closer to the shape of the human body, instead of forcing the body to adapt to the instrument!') And in fact that is precisely what we tried to do.

The last reason is philosophical and relates to our belief that the role of industry in our consumer society must be dynamic and creative . . . In short, we want the Alessofono to prove that it isn't true that the entire consumer world should be reduced to standardised large-scale manufacturing, whether that means the advanced automation of Japan's manufacturers or Eastern European price dumping. On the contrary, if small-scale producers truly respect the traditions of high quality craftsmanship, they will undoubtedly assume their own unique identity, and therefore their own place in the current complex world of consumer products . . . *Alberto Alessi*

The Alessofono is a contralto saxophone, almost entirely handmade in black chrome brass. Each instrument is dated and numbered and features gold-plated decorations and writing on the bell. The seal set on the front of the chiver is in red coral and gold.

The project, which began in the spring of 1989, led to the presentation of the first Alessofono in September 1993. Each instrument was handmade by Roberto Zolla in Quarna Sotto, successor of the original company, Rampone & Cazzani (1818), licensed by FAO Alessi and designed by Alessandro Mendini with Christina Hamel, with Luca Di Volo and Davide Mosconi as consultants.

This project is still in a developmental stage and subject to further technical modifications. So far the main technical and structural innovations include:

• The orientation of the key for the right hand is opposite to that on traditional saxophones to ensure the highest level of synergy between the levers of the two fulcrums for the fingers/keys (adapted to follow the natural movement of the fingers).

• The key of C sharp in the bass has a compensating mechanism following the movement of the palm that frees the pinky and allows the musician to play the following trills: C sharp/B and C sharp/B flat. This is why the holes in the bell and the hole on the curve have been moved to the left side of the instrument.

• The elongated shape of the keys was also modified on the basis of ergonomic needs to improve the adaptation of the finger tips and to change the length of the run required, and providing a wide range of articulations similar to those possible with piano keys.

• The more rigid, straight and vertical shape of the bell and chiver was designed to enhance the sound.

OPPOSITE: The Alessofono displayed by Alberto Alessi and Alessandro Mendini with the 'Proust' chair designed by Alessandro Mendini

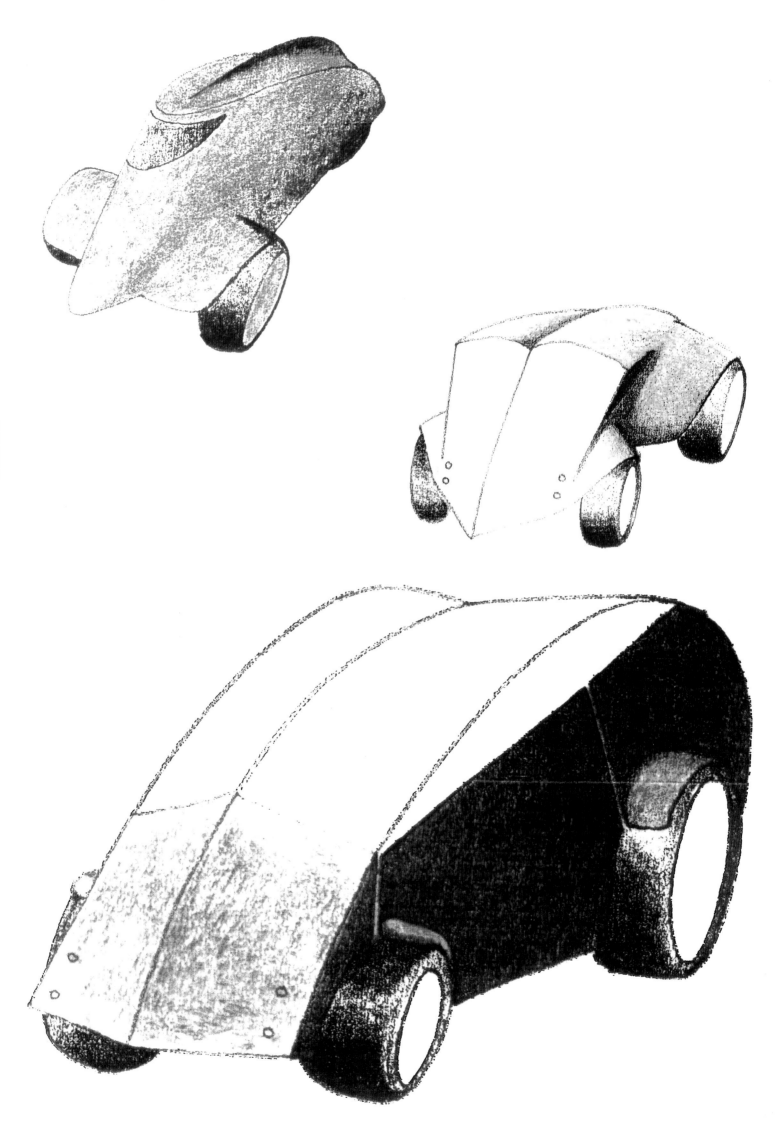

ALESSIMOBILE

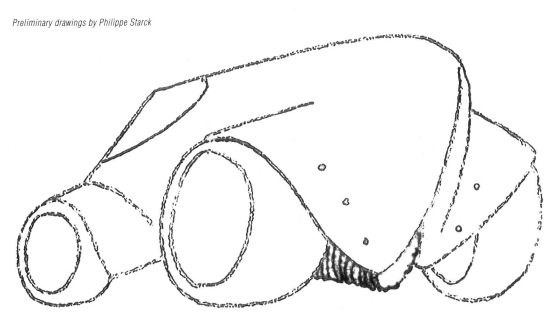

For years I have been sick of the attitude of the international producers of utilitarian cars: I find them increasing tired, boring, without spirit and without emotion. I have therefore decided to launch my Dream Car project.

I wish to show them how it would be possible to escape from the vicious circle of pure car-manufacturing technique (and from copying each other) and leave more room for creativity. I wish to conceive and realise a car which is entirely new, poetic, full of emotion!

Even though small (it must be a wind-up car, remember the toy cars of our fathers, and capable of being realised in painted tin) I am looking for a big idea, which of course should not look at the technical side but purely at the form of the car. In addition it must play a trick on them . . . When we have made the object, I wish to make a present of it to PDG Fiat, Renault, Ford, VW etc . . . It will also constitute the curious paradox of a wind-up car which will serve as an example to real cars, something which in reality normally happens the other way round, the miniature cars being the reproductions of cars which are bigger and 'real'.

To my mind it is the right project for you, Philippe, I'm sure you can understand and work on it (and, by the way, it is also a project which could lead to large sales) . . .

The project also has sentimental value for me, with the memory of the legendary toy car factory of Candido Cardini, active at Omegna between 1921 and 1929, with its extraordinary production which is today highly valued by the collector (curious: this factory had to close after nine years because Candido never wanted to raise his sale prices).   *Extract from a letter from Alberto Alessi to Philippe Starck, 18 September 1990*

Preliminary drawings by Philippe Starck

THIS IS NOT A PIPE

DANIEL WEIL

 I can remember exactly when the story of Alessi started for me. It was in 1979 when I was visiting the studio of Ettore Sottsass in Milan, and saw 'on the drawing board' his condiment set in glass and stainless steel later to become an international best seller for Alessi. On the same trip to Milan I encountered an Alessi object for the first time in Richard Sapper's Expresso coffee maker, an object so iconic in appearance and so representative of material reality that although I was already familiar with its photographic image I was taken completely by surprise by its copper-plated handle, smooth in texture and matt in finish, in contrast to its highly polished stainless steel body. It demonstrated both formal and material inspiration. Sapper's work carried with it all the design lessons about form and proportion but seemed to say so much else besides.

Alessi came to international prominence in the early 1980s with the Tea and Coffee Piazza, a series by eleven international architects, which established the role of the company as a kind of ideological carrier representing new forms of Postmodernism in the artifact – and impersonating a new architectural scale and style. This coincided with the launch of the Apple Macintosh and both have had an effect on the design process: each symbolises Postmodernism for designers in different ways. There is such a material presence in its objects that one could describe Alessi as providing material evidence of the traditional form-giving values of design in an age of information technology. Whether skilled or unskilled in software, all designers can aspire to the kind of tactile and sensory territory Alessi occupies. The fiction Alessi embraces is not the total or virtual fiction of technology – it is human and cultural fiction and everyone can participate. The material objects of Alessi touch you – as opposed to you just touching them.

For me, as for many people, Alessi products started as a series of images; but those images have succeeded in transforming themselves into real things with a genuine physical presence – and they have also found their way onto the most unexpected shelves. To see Alessi objects in shops that had never before engaged in design culture was a culture shock in itself. The sight of Michael Graves' Bird Kettle in branches of John Lewis in Britain in the mid-1980s was truly something to behold.

Alessi, then, has made a long and fantastic journey of communication – from a professional equipment brand

selling to the hotel trade in Italy (using a thoroughly modern material, stainless steel) to become an international phenomenon of Postmodern design. The internationalisation of the company is one of the most important dimensions of its recent history. The company is rooted in a culture of artisan manufacture dating back to the 1920s and the early production of trays and coffee pots in nickel-plated and silver-plated brass. The company served its apprenticeship in the 1950s and 1960s making high-quality catering utensils and vessels with an anonymous aesthetic of service which highlighted an aspirational quality of material and manufacture. In the 1970s, the rise of High-Tech style turned stainless steel Alessi products into chic, desirable objects. So by the time Alessi started to make the last lap of its journey into the international limelight in the 1980s, it did so from a commanding position in the hotel trade and with considerable experience of setting precise briefs and developing close working relationships with designers.

What Alessi has experienced as a company over the past decade conforms to the Roland Barthes notion of the Postmodern age as 'the civilisation of the image'. The company is itself a phenomenon of communication, a reflection of the speed of information transfer and of the proliferation of the colour image. Before Memphis, this media explosion had never before been experienced in design. But after the Memphis launch in 1981, as the heavily replicated 'new look' was transmitted in print and on screen around the world, the rules of the game changed. The explosion of new magazines, newspapers and TV channels removed design boundaries between countries in a way hitherto unseen. Ideas and styles went bouncing back and forth with a journalistic vigour and only skin-deep editorial scrutiny. The difference with Alessi, as a key part of the Italian media story, was that it was not a fictional character – there was substance to its presence because it was established as a manufacturer and had built its expertise around a solid skill: quality stainless steel production. This is an offer the company has never revoked. It respects its own skill.

I like to see Alessi as a contemporary version of the Vienna Werkstätte, a place where architects and designers can go to explore fresh concepts and thoughts. With notable success, Alessi created an environment which has given a final flourish to architecture as a generalist profession. It cultivated the renaissance design spirit of the Italian maestros – Achille Castiglioni, Alessandro Mendini, Aldo

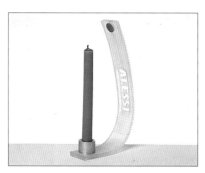

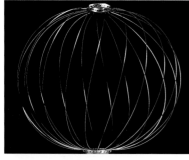

Rossi and Ettore Sottsass. That climate is now subtly changing: the new generation of people Alessi is commissioning tend to be more conventionally trained designers. But it is important to recognise the way in which Alessi allowed the architect to assume an intellectual position at the centre of material culture in the 1980s.

The first expression of this was Aldo Rossi's 'La Conica' of 1982, an uncompromising vision of small architecture exhibiting the same post-'79 Venice Biennale confidence as the Tea and Coffee Piazza series. It was at Venice in 1979 that Postmodernism was presented to the world. Rossi's work here seemed to offer the same heroic gesture: all the elements of modern design were reflected in the stainless steel body, yet it reminded you of something else.

By the time the Alessi Bird Kettle of 1985, designed by Michael Graves, was launched, the idea of an Alessi product as (in Alberto Alessi's words) 'a container for transgression' was well-established. Rules are there to be transgressed, says Alberto. Graves certainly broke all the rules. It is a hundred per cent tongue-in-cheek process which has been conceived and developed with great seriousness. It is not a piece of Postmodernism, it has Pop values in communication.

Although there were some figurative elements in the Tea and Coffee Piazza series, the Bird Kettle was Alessi's first attempt to put a figurative object into mass production. Before then, everything the company produced had been abstract, as befits the use of an authentically modern material. The Graves kettle is probably the one object people outside the design world can readily recognise and identify. It achieved fame and notoriety. As a number one hit, it opened up the culture of Alessi.

In between the architect-designers Rossi and Graves came Richard Sapper with his 1983 kettle to add a new layer of meaning to Alessi products by transgressing and infringing the language of design. Sapper's kettle is a product of enormous impact which quite literally talks to you. There is a mixed language of materials – a wavy plastic handle crowns a prodigiously austere steel dome. This is a steamboat that can whistle like a locomotive. The spout has the triggering action of a gun for loading and pouring water. The gun barrel and the pan flute are the whistle. The kettle speaks a language beyond function, compacting figuration into abstraction – a sort of 'figurative abstraction'.

So Sapper's object took its special place in the Alessi catalogue which, if you examine it today, has taken on the characteristics of an archeological dig through a century of design. All the different strata are showing, stretching back from Postmodernism through the Modern Movement, to the Bauhaus and Arts and Crafts, right back in fact to Christopher Dresser who is widely acknowledged as the world's first industrial designer. All the connections are made, yet the Alessi catalogue is bound to confuse. On the

one hand it upholds the principles of *Gutform* and shows a mastery of abstraction; yet it is also the epitome of new design, representing a period of figuration and a pluralism that is with us to stay.

It is the dream of the academic to motivate students to innovate, to find inspiration, to develop linguistic communication and to aim for technical excellence. Design students initially find themselves outside the real design experience – the design citadel, if you like – because of youth, lack of knowledge or experience. An Alessi project is like a Trojan Horse. Students can climb inside and when it opens up they find themselves inside the citadel. An Alessi student project opens doors for everyone involved.

The academic wants to contextualise design to give the process meaning and provide a clarity for students to learn and discover. The quintessential Alessi product as a 'container for transgression' – moving from one room to another, one material to another, and one context to another (from kitchen utensil to dining room status) – is in many ways a mirror image of the educational experience which must also shift its contextual boundaries and make fresh connections. Design education must also transgress to progress, although through phased evolution, not revolution for its own sake.

In developing a new language of communication – which is one of the most important aims for industrial design education – Alessi has shown great ambition and visual courage. When I was appointed Professor of Industrial Design at the Royal College of Art, London, in 1991, I was determined to find project vehicles which would enable me to teach the fundamentals of communication, representation and interpretation in design in a spirit of open-mindedness, experimentation and exploration. Alessi supplied that spirit – and, with it, generated a dialogue of great value between the academic and professional worlds. Alessi proved to be a magnificent catalyst, helping to set standards of creative invention which I hope will set the benchmark on the course at the RCA.

The first practical project with Alessi was entitled Alessi-Circus. It followed an RCA workshop led by Alberto Alessi at which he examined the complex and changing ideology of the kitchen object which emerged in the 1980s, paying particular attention to the cultural imagery and communicative values of an Alessi product. The circus was upheld as a metaphor for pluralism, one roof holding benneath it an enormous diversity of experiences. There is no connection between the activities of the clowns, the acrobats, the horses, the lion-tamer or doves in the circus; the only connection is between the tent and the event. As Charles Eames remarked:

In the actions of the circus people waiting to rehearse or preparing to perform, there is a quality of beauty which comes from appropriateness to a given situation. The concept of 'appropriateness', this 'how-it-should-be-ness', has equal value in the circus, in the making of art, and in science.

RCA students worked in teams on the project for twelve weeks. They cooked large meals together to explore the culture and ritual of preparing and eating food. The climax of Alessi-Circus was a performance at which new product prototypes were presented. It was a memorable event. Some of the resulting products are shown here. As the brief observed:

Everything in the Circus is pushing the possible beyond the limit. Yet, within this freewheeling licence, we find a discipline which is almost unbelievable.

The second Alessi project was shorter in duration – just six weeks – but equally intense and rewarding in terms of cultural connections and communicative strategy. Entitled IsolAlessi (Alessi Island), it adopted the Desert Island Discs concept of being physically marooned on a desert island. But instead of taking along a selection of records to the island, the student designer was asked to choose eight artifacts – basic kitchen utensils with which to enjoy an inexhaustible variety of foods on this faraway island. The

aim of the brief was to aim for a 'cultural basic' in design, without descending to the primitive or monastic. 'Simplicity without cultural devaluation' was the motto – with designs considered for their ability to synthesise culture in an economical way.

Both Alessi-Circus and IsolAlessi attracted enormous interest both inside and outside the College. They proved a great way to formalise the design pluralism that is all around us but is hard to engage on an academic level. They enabled the RCA and Alessi to join together as equals in developing a new language of communication.

As Alessi continues to incorporate new directions which are successful and appropriate, because it has a strong instinct to collect – now it includes wood, ceramics and plastic production – so it can make new products and explore the cultural background and technical possibilities of those materials. So the pluralism spreads, the collecting continues. I am pleased that the RCA has been given the opportunity to look inside this rich and complex process, to become a part of the process. I also like to think that we have given as well as received, that we have in some way enhanced the pluralism of Alessi

RIGHT FROM ABOVE: 'Balance', showing glass weights and central fruit bowl to be balanced by repositioning glass weights around its perimeter perforations (the candle is balanced by a weight underneath), Tom Lloyd and Carla Renders, 1992 (Alessi-Circus Project); 'Celebration', champagne bucket with eight glasses with bells on the end of glass stems, Peter Russell Clarke, David Farrage, Tomimatsu Kiyoshi, 1992 (Alessi-Circus Project); 'Fruit Cage', open, a spring steel cage which when compressed becomes a fruit basket, Takeshi Ishiguro, 1993 (IsolAlessi Project); 'Corruption', a wire spined metal ribcage with an elasticated closure that holds fruit (like a cornucopia), Tord Boontje, 1993 (IsolAlessi); OPPOSITE FROM ABOVE: 'Lingotto' candle and detail of wax memento (when the candle is lit and melts it rocks into a horizontal position, the wax then drips onto a specially engraved area, and can be then removed as a memento), David Leary, 1992 (Alessi-Circus Project); 'Etiquette' closed

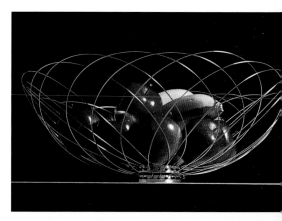

template to set formal dinner table, Sam Hecht and Wayne James, 1992 Alessi-Circus Project; 'Etiquette' open template; 'Lingotto'; 'Celebration', detail of ice cast in specialised mould to chill and stabilise champagne bottle; 'Fruit Cage', closed; 'Fifty-Fifty', the fruit tray pivots to reveal a cutting board for cheese and fruit, Michael Corsar, 1993 (IsolAlessi Project); PAGE 141 BACKGROUND IMAGE: Detail of 'Balance'; INSET 'Water and Wine Glass', a stopper plugs the hollow stem for wine drinking, when the plug is removed and positioned under the base the whole glass can be filled with water, Tord Boontje, 1993 (IsolAlessi Project); 'Water and Wine Glass' with water; 'Comedia del' Arte', domestic trolley that contains cutlery belt, condiment set, plates and glasses and all table accessories for six people, David Elliot and Stephan Reichl, 1992 (Alessi-Circus Project); 'Honey Pot' with twirler, Dan Gratiot

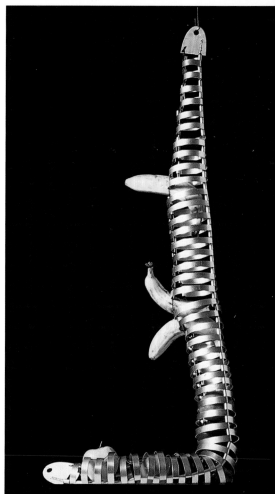

TEXT CREDITS

Alberto Alessi, 'The Design Factories: Europe's Industrial Future?' pp6-13, first delivered as a lecture at the Royal Geographical Society, London, June 1993, sponsored by Pentagram and the Design Museum.
'A Brief History', pp16-18, updated version of Laura Polinoro's text in *L'officina Alessi*, FAO spa, 1989 (trans Paolo Valli).
'Programme 8', p19, edited (with the assistance of David Liddell and Guy Marriage) from 'Un'utopia degli anni Settanta' by Patrizia Scarzella in *Il Bel Metallo*, Arcadia Edizioni, 1985 (trans Donato Persichillo).
'The Metaproject', pp20-21, edited (with the assistance of David Liddell and Guy Marriage) from a text by Laura Polinoro in *L'officina Alessi* (trans Donato Persichillo).
'The Boston Shaker and Bar Accessories', p24, edited from 'Oggetti per un professionista' in *Il Bel Metallo* (trans Donato Persichillo).
'The Serving Dish with a Bell-shaped Cover', pp24-25, edited from 'Già visto, ma nuovo' by Patrizia Scarzella in *Il Bel Metallo* (trans Donato Persichillo).
'The Condiment Set 1980-84' by Patrizia Scarzella, pp31-33, first published in *Officina Alessi*, FAO spa, 1994.
'Officina Alessi', pp44-45 first published in *Officina Alessi*.
'Objects as Precious Individuals' by Marco Migliari, pp46-49, first published in *FFF*, FAO spa, 1993.
'Kettle with a Singing Whistle', pp50-51, edited from a text by Laura Polinoro in *L'officina Alessi* (trans Donato Persichillo).
'The Project', pp54-55, edited from a text by Laura Polinoro in *L'officina Alessi* (trans Donato Persichillo).
'The Project', p57, extracts from Alberto Alessi's 'Manufacturer's Note' in *La caffettiera e pulcinella*, Alessi spa, 1987.
Frank Gehry, p60, first quoted in *Officina Alessi*.
'The Sensory Revolution', p61, by Laura Polinoro first published in *L'officina Alessi* (trans Paolo Valli).
'Cibi e Riti' by Laura Polinoro, pp67, first published in *L'officina Alessi* (trans Paolo Valli).
'The Pasta-set' by Laura Polinoro, p68, first published in *L'officina Alessi*, (trans Paolo Valli).
'Nuovo Milano Cutlery' text by Alberto Alessi and extract from Ettore Sottsass, p71, first published in *L'officina Alessi* (trans Donato Persichillo).
'La Cintura di Orione' by Alberto Alessi, pp72-73, first published in *La Cintura di Orione: Catalogue of Cooking Utensils*.
'Falstaf' by Laura Polinoro, p74, first published in *L'officina Alessi* (trans Donato Persichillo).
'Caccia Flatware', p77, extract from a text first published in *Officina Alessi*.
'La Tavola di Babele', p78, first published in *Officina Alessi*.
'Archivi', p82, first published in *Officina Alessi*.
'Antologia Alessi', p83, first published in *Officina Alessi*.
'La Casa della Felicità' by Laura Polinoro, p90, first published in *L'officina Alessi* (trans Donato Persichillo).
'Cronotime', p92, extracts from 'A Precious Automobile Designer Designs a Clock' by Enzo Frateili which first appeared in *Alessi Clocks Officina Watches*, FAO spa, 1993.
'Optic', p93, from 'The "Global Designer"' by Ugo La Pietra which first appeared in *Alessi Clocks Officina Watches*.
Michael Graves, p94, first quoted in *Alessi Clocks Officina Watches*.
Robert Venturi, p95, first quoted in *Alessi Clocks Officina Watches*.
Philippe Starck, p96, first quoted in *Alessi Clocks Officina Watches*.
Shigeru Uchida, p97, first quoted in *Alessi Clocks Officina Watches*.
Richard Sapper, p99 first quoted in *Alessi Clocks Officina Watches*.
'The Clock or the Moment' by Aldo Rossi, p98, first published in *Alessi Clocks Officina Watches*.
'Tekton', p100, from a text by Volker Fischer entitled 'Highrise Application: The Architect as an Aesthetician of the Metropolis', first published in *Alessi Clocks Officina Watches*.
Mario Botta, p101, first quoted in *Alessi Clocks Officina Watches*.

'The Projects', p103, Alberto Alessi first quoted in *L'officina Alessi* (trans Donato Persichillo).
Philippe Starck, pp104-05, first quoted in *L'officina Alessi* (trans Donato Persichillo).
'Twergi' by Laura Polinoro, p111, first published in *L'officina Alessi* (trans Donato Persichillo).
'Project for a Revival of the Artisan Tradition' by Patrizia Scarzella, p114, first published in *Vasi Comunicanti*, Idea Books Edizioni, 1990.
'La Bella Tavola and My Beautiful China' by Ettore Sottsass, p117, first published in *Alessi Tendentse: La Bella Tavola and My Beautiful China*, FAO spa, 1993.
'The "100% Make-up"' by Alessandro Mendini, p118, first published in *100% Make up: Alessandro Mendini and La Fabbrica Estetica*, Alessi Tendentse, 1992.
'The Centro Studi Alessi' by Laura Polinoro, p123, first published in *Rebus sic . . .*, FAO, 1991.
'Memory Containers' by Laura Polinoro, p125, first published in *Rebus sic . . .*
'Towards an Awareness of the Things we Buy' by Alberto Alessi, p127, first published in *Rebus sic . . .*
'Family Follows Fiction' texts by Alberto Alessi and Laura Polinoro, pp131-32, first published in *FFF Family Follows Fiction*, FAO spa, 1993.
'Alessofono', p137, text first published in *Officina Alessi*.

SELECT BIBLIOGRAPHY

Books

Alessi, Alberto and Gozzi, Alberto *La Cintura di Orione*, Alessi spa, 1987.
Alessi, Alberto and Gozzi, Alberto, *La Cucina Alessi*, Alessi spa, 1988.
Alessi, Alberto *Not in Production/Next to Production*, Alessi spa, 1988.
Dalisi, Riccardo *L'oggetto eroticomiko*, FAO Alessi, 1991.
Mendini, Alessandro *Paesaggio Casalingo*, Alessi spa, 1981.
Medagliani, Eugenio and Gosetti, Fernanda, *Pastario or Atlas of Italian Pastas*, Alessi spa, 1989.
Polinoro, Laura *L'officina Alessi*, FAO spa 1989.
Rossi, Aldo *'La Conica', 'La Cupola' e altre cafetiere*, Alessi spa, 1984, (3rd ed 1988).
Scarzella, Patrizia *Il Bel Metallo*, Arcadia Edizioni, 1985.
Scarzella, Patrizia *Vasi Comunicanti*, Idea Books Edizioni, 1990.
Solaro, Giovanni *La Giostra delle Libellule*, Libreria Il Punto, 1992.
Sottsass, Ettore *Esercizio Formale 1979*, Alessi spa, 1989.
100% Make up: Alessandro Mendini and La Fabbrica Estetica, FAO, 1992.
Christopher Dresser, FAO spa, 1991
Cibi e Riti, Alessi spa, 1991.
FFF Family Follows Fiction Workshop 1991/1993, FAO spa, 1993.
La Caffettiera e Pulcinella, Alessi spa, 1987.
Philippe Starck, Alessi spa, 1990.
Rebus sic . . ., FAO, 1991.
Tea and Coffee Piazza, Alessi spa, 1983.

Catalogues

Alessi Falstaf, Alessi spa, 1989.
Alessi Production Yearbook, FAO spa, 1994.
Alessi Tendentse: La Bella Tavola and My Beautiful China, FAO spa, 1993.
Alessi Clocks/Officina Watches, FAO spa, 1993.
La Cintura di Orione: Catalogue of Cooking Utensils, FAO spa, 1991.
La Casa della Felicità, FAO spa, 1991.
Officina Alessi, FAO spa, 1994.
Twergi Catalogue no 6/1994, Piazza Battista 1865 Srl, 1994.